Pilgrim's England

We are the pilgrims, master; we shall go
Always a little further. . . .

James Elroy Flecker, *Hassan*.

Longman Travellers Series

Pilgrim's England
A personal journey

WILLIAM PURCELL
Line drawings by Trevor Stubley

Longman *London and New York*

Longman Group Limited,

Longman House,
Burnt Mill, Harlow, Essex, U.K.

First published 1981

British Library Cataloguing in Publication Data

Purcell, William
    Pilgrim's England. – (Longman travellers series).
    1. England – Description and travel – 1971 –
    2. Christian pilgrims and pilgrimages – England
    3. Christian shrines – England
    I. Title
    914.1'04'857   PA632   80-40396

    ISBN 0-582-50290-X

Set in 10/12pt V-I-P Palatino
Printed and bound in Great Britain by
William Clowes (Beccles) Limited,
Beccles and London

Contents

Acknowledgements

We are grateful to the following for permission to reproduce copyright material:

Penguin Books Ltd. for extracts from pp. 44, 47, 127, 181, 188, 208–212, 239–240, 252 and 272 of *A History of the English Church and People* by Bede translated by Leo Sherley-Price (Penguin Classics, Revised edition, 1968). Copyright © Leo Sherley-Price, 1955, 1968.

Introduction:
Before setting out

In an old book in the library of Worcester Cathedral is a print of a pilgrim. He dates from the late fifteenth century, and so from a time towards the end of the great pilgrimage tide which flowed across Europe for many centuries. The pilgrim's costume was significant. He wore a long gown, or habit: a scallop shell sometimes adorned the brim of his hat: in his left hand he carried a staff. Over his right shoulder there was a wallet. The shell indicated that he had made pilgrimage to the shrine of St James, or Santiago, at Compostela in north-eastern Spain. This, traditionally held to be the burial-place of St James the Apostle, was a pilgrimage centre then, as indeed it still is to this day. The wallet was the sign of a wayfaring man. Maybe, though we cannot tell, this individual had made pilgrimage to Jerusalem, the ultimate goal of such travels. The redoubtable Wife of Bath in Chaucer's *Canterbury Tales* made that tough journey no less than three times, as well as having been to Compostela and various other places in Europe. 'She knew much of wandering by the way', as Chaucer so rightly says. The pilgrim routes of the Middle Ages were thronged with such figures, up hill and down dale, on foot and on horseback. Some features in the pilgrim costume are remembered in a lovely verse of Sir Walter Ralegh's *The Passionate Man's Pilgrimage*, written years after the custom in its popular form had died away:

> Give me my scallop shell of quiet,
> My staff of faith to walk upon,
> My scrip of joy, immortal diet,
> My bottle of salvation,
> My gown of glory, hopes true gage,
> And thus I'll take my pilgrimage.

It is good equipment for such a journey. For ideally, a pilgrim is one who wishes to find a religious dimension in his travels, and is prepared to set out in the spirit of those of olden times who went along, like Chaucer's party to Canterbury, not only for shared companionship and the safety of numbers, but also for what they saw as spiritual benefit. This could take many forms. A pilgrimage could be an act of penitence or of thanksgiving. It could be a search for healing. It could be simply an act of devotion. It could be the fulfilment of a desire to wander.

This very ancient motive is found in all peoples in all ages; sometimes unexpectedly. In Russia as late as the nineteenth century there were always peasants on the roads to Kasan, Kiev and Novgorod. These are the simple folk whom Tolstoy in *War and Peace* shows the devout Princess Maria receiving secretly, because her rationalist father disapproved, in the kitchen quarters of the estate mansion, and listening to their artless tales of wonders encountered along the way.

The fact is that we are all at heart pilgrims, except that we call it travel. We are all restless. The Wife of Bath today would probably be a blue-rinsed widow going round and round the world on cruise liners, or here, there and everywhere on package tours. It is difficult to avoid the impression that she had moved a long way from the idea of pilgrimage as travel religiously motivated, to that of pilgrimage simply as travel for its own sake. But the pilgrim idea is by no means dead, even if it is not consciously held. There are almost certainly more visitors, in terms of numbers, to such places as Canterbury, Winchester, Durham and many others, than there were in the Middle Ages. Walsingham on a public holiday in summer is a fantastic sight. So is York; so is St Albans; so is Holy Island, or Lindisfarne, when the tide has receded enough to let the waiting cars pass over the causeway which links that holy place to the mainland.

We are, here, in the presence of a living tradition. The fact that so many of the relics of mediaeval pilgrimage are ruins, does not mean that they do not still have power in them. It is as though, moving round a partially demolished house, we were to touch wires left dangling from a wall and receive a shock, because they are still mysteriously alive.

Pilgrims' Badges. These could be bought at most shrines during the Middle Ages, and were very popular. One (*above*) comes from the Shrine of Our Lady at Walsingham and depicts the Annunciation. The mounted figure (*below*) is that of St Thomas of Canterbury. (*Museum of London*)

The roots of pilgrimage lie far back. They have also been associated, from the earliest times, with relics, that is to say, with the physical and tangible evidences of venerated persons, like the hand of St Etheldreda, to be seen to this day in the Catholic church of that dedication in Ely, Cambridgeshire, or the head of St Chad which once was held in a reliquary in Lichfield Cathedral and now is in the Catholic cathedral in Birmingham. Relics, moreover, have a continuing appeal, and claims for their powers are still being made, sometimes in unexpected places. I was startled, in the course of travels made for this book, to discover a human hand in a glass tabernacle on a side altar in the Catholic church of St Oswald at Ashton in Makerfield, in Lancashire. It was the right hand, shrivelled by burning, of the martyr Edmund Arrowsmith, a Jesuit priest executed at Lancaster in 1628 and declared a saint in 1970. Healing powers are claimed for this relic, a recent case being that of a Liverpool man with lung cancer who was apparently cured when the hand was brought to him. Without a recognition of this kind of belief the pilgrimage cult cannot be understood.

This was particularly true when the purpose of pilgrimage was to seek for bodily healing. It was as though, to the pilgrim who sought relief at the shrine of a saint, the bones they contained were 'radioactive', in the sense that, from close proximity to them, healing power could be derived. The apertures to be seen in some ancient shrines such as, to take a famous example, that of Edward the Confessor in Westminster Abbey, or the obscure St Wite in the church at Whitchurch Canonicorum, in Dorset, allowed pilgrims to touch the tomb, thus getting as close as possible to the source of the healing influence. There is something which calls to most of us in this idea, however stoutly we would deny it. If this be not so how is it that, to take one instance, the waters of the River Jordan are widely held to have some particular influence of their own? I have myself noticed, when leading modern Holy Land pilgrimages, how all sorts of people, including sceptics, will want to get out of the coach in order to paddle in that not very impressive-looking stream, and take bottles of its water back home. Why should this be so? Because Jesus was baptised in the river. It is a perfect example of holiness by association, one of the master-motivations behind pilgrimage. What is more, it can spring up unexpectedly. St Paul himself might well have been surprised by what happened in Ephesus as a result of his activity in that city, as recorded in the nineteenth chapter of the Acts of the Apostles: 'God did extraordinary miracles by the hands of Paul, so that handkerchiefs or aprons were carried away from his body to the sick, and diseases left them and the evil spirits came out of them.' There is an echo here of the mantle of Elijah story in the Old Testament, where Elisha finds such miraculous powers in the garment that he is able to part the Jordan by striking the waters with it. Similarly, the grave of Elisha himself develops healing properties, so that a dead man placed in it revives as soon as his body touches the prophet's bones.

We are now in a position to see how the pilgrim idea developed in Christian history. Its roots can be understood once it has been recognised that, growing in the ancient soil of magic, they have always been fertilised by the equally ancient human desire to clothe beliefs in form and substance. Judging by the above passage from Acts, it is clear that the origins of Christian pilgrimage are to be found in the earliest days of the faith. It would be a short step from discovering miraculous properties in objects handled by Paul, to going on pilgrimage to see them and to benefit from their powers. This is the pattern of many later pilgrimage cults.

The next noticeable stage arose out of persecution in the early Church. This, often involving death for the faith, produced the bodies of martyrs, and veneration of these bodies which, reverently gathered together and buried with honour in such places as the Catacombs in Rome, readily enough led to pilgrimages to them. A description of the martyrdom of Polycarp, Bishop of Smyrna, dating from the second century, describes his relics, in other words, his remains, as 'more valuable than precious stones and finer than refined gold'.

This cult gathered impetus when, following the acceptance of Christianity by the Emperor Constantine, leading to imperial favour for Christians, many former pagans flocked into the Church. These, bringing with them the customs of their pagan world, where the worship of images had been a familiar practice, took readily to the worship of relics – indeed, too readily. Its dangers, so easily leading to idolatry, were made plain by some of the early fathers of the Church. St Augustine, for one, stated that the reasons why the bodies of the saints should be venerated was not for their own sake; but for that of the Christ whom they had served. The ever present tendency of the pilgrimage cult to drift into the area of superstition thus began very early, as did the opposition to it.

A remarkable woman, possibly the most notable relic hunter of all time, now comes upon the scene. This was Helena – later St Helena – mother of the Emperor Constantine. A zealous supporter of the Christian cause, she visited the Holy Land towards the end of her life. She it was who had, according to legend, the whereabouts of the true Cross disclosed to her in a dream, as lying under what is now the Church of the Holy Sepulchre in Jerusalem. She also founded basilicas in Bethlehem, and on the Mount of Olives. Her purpose was to discover, and to mark with a church, as many as possible of the sites associated with the Gospel story. Where she led many followed. Where she discovered sites and relics, others soon began to claim the discovery of more. The Holy Land became the Christian Mecca, as it still is and as, increasingly, more discoveries were placed in more and more churches. Meanwhile, other pilgrimage centres were developing in Europe. Rome was rich in relics, including the bones of Peter and Paul. Every country developed its own. Almost every locality developed its own. The demand for relics became so great that the practice began of dividing up the bodies of saints in order that portions might be shared out. And when the Second Council of Nicaea in 787 ruled that no church should be consecrated without relics placed under its altar the need for them became more pressing than ever. This may well account for the curious fact that some of the major relics appear to have been regarded as self-multiplying. How else could there be, for instance, a House of the Holy Family in Loreto in Italy, and also at Walsingham in England?

The Crusades, which vastly encouraged pilgrimage to the Holy Land, were a further stage in the development of the practice of pilgrimage. To 'take the Cross' was to make the journey to the holy places, and many thousands, in crusader times and later, did so. The sign of a palm branch carried by some was an indication that they had been as far as Jericho – hence the term for such pilgrims, palmers. The routes became well established, with accommodation and transport organised along the ways across Europe. There is a quaint glimpse of these folk struggling with language difficulties in a work printed by Caxton about 1483. *Dialogues in French and English* was a phrase book, originally French–Flemish, compiled in Bruges in the first half of the fourteenth century for the use of pilgrims. Caxton added the English. A pilgrim party arrives at a lodging and one of them thus addresses the hostess:

'Dame, God be here!'
'Fellow, ye be welcome.'
'May I have a bed here within?'
'Yea, well and clenley, even though ye were twelve, and all on horseback.'
'Nay, but we be three. Is there to eat here within?'
'Yea, enough; God be thanked.'
'Bring it to us. Give hay to the horses, and straw them well.'

There were three principal religious motives for pilgrimage. The first was to seek forgiveness of sins. For a sin confessed the Church would prescribe a penance, and in the Middle Ages it

Fifteenth-century pilgrims arriving at an inn. They sleep naked in a common bed. (*Glasgow University Library*)

became an increasing custom to use pilgrimages for this purpose, which at once made something special of a pilgrim. He became a person set aside from ordinary life because his journey had a religious dimension. So he travelled light and unarmed, carrying the staff which was a sign of his pilgrim status. If he felt his sins heavy upon him he might go barefoot as an act of penitence. Some people ascending barefoot the stony track up Croagh Patrick, in Ireland may be seen doing this very thing nowadays. Or the pilgrim might have gone fettered, or wearing a hair shirt. The great thing was to be a *poor* pilgrim, working out the hard way of salvation through forgiveness of sins.

This was the ideal, and was truly attained by many. But inevitably complications and even debasements appeared. The use of indulgences, and especially the sale of them was beyond question a contributing factor. An indulgence was a certificate to the effect that the bearer had received a remission of a period in purgatory. A plenary indulgence indicated exemption from all temporal punishment due to sin. The right to issue them was at first limited to the papacy. Thus, Urban II promised plenary indulgence to all offering themselves for the First Crusade. Eventually, others acquired the rights to sell indulgences, including the guardians of many famous shrines. In course of time those in charge of lesser shrines likewise acquired a right, which was obviously of great value. By the time of the Middle Ages the practice had proliferated exceedingly. It had also become astonishingly mixed up. So it became possible to send substitutes on pilgrimage, even to leave a bequest to pay for a substitute pilgrim to claim plenary indulgence by travelling to a shrine and praying there for the soul of the individual who had left money for this purpose. There is an interesting entry in the will of a certain William Ball of Elsing of Norfolk dated 1480: 'I Will and bequeath to have two divers pilgrimages for me to St Thomas of Canterbury and one to St Thomas of Westacre', the last an image of St Thomas housed in a chapel dedicated to him in a Norfolk Augustinian priory. Eventually, it became possible to buy indulgences direct without making a penance pilgrimage, either in person or by a substitute.

A further development was the appearance of professional pardoners, who travelled around selling cut-price indulgences. There is a notable portrait of one of this breed in the prologue to Chaucer's *Canterbury Tales*, who, in addition to his indulgences, carried as stock the veil worn by the Blessed Virgin, a piece of the sail from St Peter's boat, and a collection of pigs' bones which he could pass off as those of saints. This practice of the professional pardoner was finally prohibited by Pope Pious V in 1567.

The second of these three principal motives for pilgrimage was to seek physical relief and, if possible cure at the shrines of saints and at other holy places. It will be encountered frequently at the shrines described in this journey. Nor is it necessarily to be set aside as mere gullibility on the part of our pilgrim forebears. Is it possible that all of the tens of thousands of suffering people, many grossly handicapped and crippled and living in an age of the most rudimentary medical knowledge, who sought help in this way, were all deluded? Testimonies of the time as, for instance, in those splendid mediaeval windows in Canterbury which illustrate cures effected at the shrine of St Thomas strongly suggest otherwise. Obviously, some cures were psychosomatic, some were auto-suggestive, some did not happen; but were thought to have done so. The subject is highly complex, certainly too complicated to be brushed aside.

Thirdly, there was the motive of straightforward devotion. A pilgrimage was, as it still can be, a religious exercise; doing something for God, or at any rate doing something which was deeply felt to be good for the soul. In a way it was a personal demonstration against the everyday world of getting and spending, a great gesture of 'getting away from it all', or to put it another way, of abnegation. There were many men and women who in this way devoted themselves entirely to the pilgrim life, wandering from shrine to shrine until they died. This personal dedication is the other side of the coin of pilgrimage from that which bears evidence of the undoubted abuses which arose from the cult. So against the image of the villainous pardoner should always be set that of the humble pilgrims who in their way, chose to be fools for God. Wherever we come upon their traces, in stairs their feet have worn or in objects their hands have rubbed, it is well to remember that not all of them were deluded, or had gone along just for the fun of travel and the enjoyment of telling tall tales about it afterwards.

Then, quite suddenly, it was all over. The world of mediaeval pilgrimage, with much else, vanished at the coming of great new concepts of faith and belief at the Reformation. The process had been in progress for some time. The tide of pilgrimage had begun to ebb long before 1536, the year which saw the Act for the Dissolution of the Monasteries laid before Parliament. The number of pilgrims to the greater shrines had been gradually dwindling for many years, and an undercurrent of criticism of much that they represented had increased. Many within the system had sensed for some time the impending change. 'This year many dreadful gales', wrote a canon of Butley Priory, Suffolk, in his chronicle of the year 1534. 'Much rain, lightning and thunder, especially in summer time, and at odd times throughout the year; also divers mortal fevers, and the charity of many people grows cold; no love, not the least devotion remains in the people; but rather many false opinions.' Or so he thought, not knowing that he, and all he stood for, were shortly to be carried away by the gale of the world. But it was done, on the whole, gently as regards the individuals involved. Many elderly monks were pensioned off, having been ready to go, anyway. Others carried on in different guises. The last Prior of Worcester, for instance, became the cathedral's first Dean. And the wills of the period reflect the fact that many nuns of gentle family settled down quite comfortably with nephews and nieces.

The real casualties were the pilgrim shrines. That of St Alban was broken into a thousand pieces. The image of the Walsingham Virgin was burnt at Smithfield, together with many others. The dismantling of the great shrine of the North, St Cuthbert's at Durham, and the emptying of his coffin is a strange story which we shall come to in the course of this journey. A huge work of demolition was accomplished in a surprisingly short time, so that soon the grass was growing along the old pilgrim routes, and the figures which had thronged them had vanished into the past.

But they have left many fascinating traces. Nor has pilgrim's England ended with them, but is alive and well and awaiting whoever wishes to wander along its many ways, finding among its treasures things new and old. The purpose of recording this personal pilgrimage is to try and share with others something of the intense pleasure which these journeyings through from spring to autumn have given me. The intention has been not tourism but exploration and the motive is not to 'do' as many places as possible; but to enter in some depth into the true meaning of those which have been selected.

Inevitably, much has had to be omitted. But even if we cannot see all, we can at any rate see much. For it is always true that

> . . . there is good news yet to hear, and fine things to be seen,
> Before we go to Paradise by way of Kensal Green.

CHAPTER 1

St Albans and the Fens

England's first Martyr
Ely – St Etheldreda

St Alban

It was a bright, sunny morning when I arrived in St Albans. In one of the huts alongside the excavations in progress for the foundation of a new chapter-house, American girl students were sorting out human bones, long femurs, skulls yellowed with age. The Dean told me how excited they all were at having recently uncovered the burial-place of the father of Nicholas Breakspear who, in 1154 elected Pope, took the name of Adrian IV and was the only Englishman from that day to this ever to be Bishop of Rome.

Inside the great abbey and cathedral church which, after Winchester, has the longest nave in England, a party of school-children working on a project were gazing earnestly at the mediaeval paintings on the pillars. Those on the west sides of the pillars in the upper panels portray the Crucifixion: in the lower, the Virgin Mary. On the south there are St Christopher, patron saint of pilgrims, St Thomas of Canterbury, the most popular of them all, and St Osyth, possibly the least known of all. An obscure lady said to have been the daughter of a Mercian chieftain, she was forcibly married to a king of the East Saxons, left him, founded a convent on the east coast and was murdered by pirates, a bizarre sequence of events somehow typical of this extraordinary place. There is also Edward the Confessor. The face of St Thomas has been mysteriously rubbed out. These impressive paintings, cleaned in 1955, were the work of a school

of artists famous when St Albans Abbey was a very great place indeed.

It still is. Looked at from outside it dominates the hill on which it stands and the town clustered around. The occasional red London bus in the streets is a reminder of how near, and yet how distinct from the capital, is this town. It is in fact 21 miles, as shown on Roman road maps, along Watling Street, the highway going north. There was a crossing point here with another important road, the Icknield Way. It was an average day's journey by horse in Roman times. The bricks in the tower are twice as old as the ancient structure itself, for they are Roman, taken from Verulamium, a chartered Roman city, or *municipium*, established in A.D. 50. Later builders of the abbey, first Saxon, then Norman, used the ruins, by their times tumbled down and overgrown, as a convenient quarry for the stone they needed. So St Albans is in part a Romano-British building. And the reason why it is unquestionably the most logical place to begin a journey into pilgrim England is that here, on this very hill where the cathedral stands, there took place the first Christian martyrdom in Britain.

The victim was Alban; probably a soldier, certainly a Roman. Because of this he had the privilege accorded to citizens of the Empire of execution by the sword rather than by one of the frightful methods, such as crucifixion, or death in the arena by wild beasts, which could befall members of subject races. This was the man who, in the year 209, was taken up the hill from the town below, across the little River Ver, still flowing in its valley, to an open space covered with grass, probably the site of a Roman cemetery. There his head was struck off and the story of St Albans began. Why this event took place, and what that story in course of time became, have both to be discovered before later developments of this huge abbey, at one time the most highly regarded monastery in England, can be understood.

It is worth while to pause a moment, and think about that date – the year 209. Until fairly recently the martyrdom of Alban was placed later, around 303, during the reign of the Emperor Diocletian. However, later discoveries have made it clear that the year was in fact 209, and the reigning Emperor Severus, a notable

St Alban's Abbey, crowning the hill upon which the martyrdom of Alban took place, above the Roman City of Verulamium. (*A. F. Kersting*)

persecutor of Christians. The significance of this is impressive. It means that, if the crucifixion of Christ took place in A.D. 30 Alban suffered in his name not more than 179 years afterwards, which places him not much further off that happening in time than we are from the Battle of Waterloo. It also means that there must have been a Christian presence in Verulamium by then. When Sir Mortimer Wheeler the archaeologist excavated the site in the 1930s, he did not find a basilica, or church. There was certainly a theatre, now uncovered; there was a forum. There were several temples. But there is some evidence for a Christian grave chapel in the Roman cemetery outside the London gate of the city.

This is what gives this place its particular fascination, because, beyond by far any other place in this island, it takes us closest in time to the event from which Christianity itself stems. Everything else seen on this journey – shrines, pilgrims ways, holy wells – all date from centuries later. So St Albans really is where it all began, and that is what makes it such a rewarding place for us to begin, too.

Who was Alban? He was almost certainly of considerable social standing. Had he not been so it is unlikely that so much importance would have been attached to his action when the effects of a wave of persecution of Christians throughout the Roman Empire reached this place. Alban, who was not himself a Christian, gave shelter to a fugitive priest. By this priest Alban was baptised. Shortly afterwards, when troops came to his house to arrest the fugitive, Alban, changing clothes with him, gave himself up in his stead. He was then taken before the examining magistrate and required, as was customary, to make sacrifice to the gods, usually by sprinkling incense on an altar. This he refused to do, claiming that he now owed allegiance to a higher power. He was then condemned to death. The date was 22 June 209, still marked in the cathedral by an annual Rose Service.

A fuller account is given in a manuscript kept in the National Library at Turin, a narrative which shows how, by embellishments and additions over the centuries, the cult of a saint was built up. The fact that this material lies in Turin is in itself curious. It so happened that St Columban in 583 was travelling through from Bangor in Ireland via St Albans en route for London, the Channel and then Luxeuil in the Vosges. Much impressed with the story of Alban, by then already a venerated figure, they spread it abroad. So churches dedicated to St Alban are to be found still in Savoy, sprung from the seed Columban and his party let fall. The earliest written sources originate from the fifth century, though there are hints of others earlier still. The successors of Columban, driven in the seventh century from the monastery which he had founded at Luxeuil, took refuge in northern Italy, thus coming under the protection of the Archbishopric of Turin. So the manuscript came to rest in that Italian city.

It begins: 'The Emperor Severus, who was hanging on the necks of Christians like a ravening lion and was roaring night and day against the name of Christian, sent his thugs at that time into the Province of Gaul to search for Christians.' He then crossed over to Britain, asking on arrival the ominous question: 'If in these distant parts of the world there are men who confess the name of Christ.' Severus, who well lived up to his name, was accompanied by two of his sons, Antonius Augustus and Geta, Antonius went north to York with his father the Emperor: Geta was left behind in Verulamium to carry on his father's orders for the extermination of Christians. It was into his hands that Alban fell. The manuscript continues:

When it became clear that there were very many Christians there, with his customary fury he ordered them all to be put to the sword. He pursued a cleric who was given hospitality by Alban, who put on the garment worn by the priest, and delivered himself to be killed in his stead although, according to ancient tradition, he was still a pagan.

Alban is then cross-examined:

'What is your name?'
'I am Alban.'
'Why do you give hospitality to, and protect those whom you know are Christians, men who insult the gods, who worship a man who was crucified by men. . . . Give me your answer. Offer sacrifices to Jupiter and Apollo.'

Alban replies:

'I confess Jesus Christ, the son of God, with my whole being. Those whom you call gods are idols; they are made by hands . . .'

He is then pressed again to recant, even to the extent of a promise that he will not only be continued in the post he already holds, but also benifited by marriage to a lady of senatorial rank. He refuses and then, according to custom, is flogged. Recalled before the tribunal he is once more pressed to sacrifice. This time his refusal is final. He is tortured, again as was customary, and condemned to death by the sword. The narrative goes on:

> When he came to the place appointed for his death, the executioner ran towards him with his sword drawn, begging that he, who was to have killed the martyr, should himself be punished in his stead, and threw away his sword and fell at St Alban's feet, urging him to pray to the Lord for him. As the sword lay on the ground among the other executioners, who hesitated, the holy martyr and the crowds climbed the hill, which rose with inexpressible beauty for five hundred paces from the Arena. It was clothed and coloured with various kinds of flowers. It had undoubtedly been made ready long since for the martyr; before it was consecrated with sacred blood, its natural beauty had made it like a shrine. At the top of the hill St Alban asked for a drink of water. Immediately and incredibly a perpetual spring sprang up at the martyr's feet.

The manuscript then adds that, after the executioner had delivered his stroke, his eyes fell out on to the ground. This scene is depicted in a carving, one of many, on the west side of St Alban's shrine which lies in an area of its own behind the high altar. This is a shrine which was reassembled from a thousand pieces in the nineteenth-century restoration.

On the north side of it stands a strange wooden structure, known as the watching loft, used in mediaeval times by monks appointed to guard the shrine and the many treasures left there as offerings by grateful pilgrims. The carvings round the lower edgings of this loft show homely and sometimes humorous scenes from daily life in the Middle Ages.

On the south side of the shrine is an iron grille through which pilgrims could peer. On the same side is the tomb of Humphrey, Duke of Gloucester, brother of Henry V, which is an excellent example of how persons of distinction liked to be buried near the shrines of saints, like the Black Prince at Canterbury, or King John at Worcester. Northwards of the watching loft is another reconstructed shrine, that of St Amphibulus, a name later attached by legend to the priest whom Alban sheltered. Here again is a characteristic of the growth of legend – the practice of giving names, even when they do not in fact exist, to all characters in the drama.

When Bede came to tell the Alban story in his *History of the English Church and People* it is clear that he was drawing on some version of this early source which had reached him, or been told him, in his monastery far away at Jarrow in the North. On the other hand it is clear that Bede had little idea of the nature or identity of Alban's persecutors.

In this country occurred the suffering of St Alban, of whom the Priest Fortunatus in his *Praise of Virgins*, in which he mentions all the blessed martyrs who came to God from every part of the world, says:

In fertile Britain land
Was noble Alban born.

When these unbelieving Emperors were issuing savage edicts against all Christians, Alban, as yet a pagan, gave shelter to a Christian priest fleeing from his pursuers. And when he observed this man's unbroken activity of prayer and vigil, he was suddenly touched by the grace of God and began to follow the priest's example of faith and devotion. Gradually instructed by his teaching of salvation, Alban renounced the darkness of idolatry, and sincerely accepted Christ. But when the priest had lived in his house some days, word came to the ears of the evil ruler that he lay hidden in Alban's house. Accordingly he gave orders to his soldiers to make a thorough search, and when they arrived at the martyr's house, holy Alban, wearing the priest's long cloak, at once surrendered himself in the place of his guest and teacher, and was led bound before the Judge. When Alban was brought in, the Judge happened to be standing before an altar, offering sacrifice to devils. Seeing Alban, he was furious that he had presumed to put himself in such hazard by surrendering himself to the soldiers in place of his guest.

The trial, torture and condemnation then follows much as in the Turin manuscript. The conclusion of Bede's account needs, however, to be given in his own words. It will be seen how yet

other embellishments are added to the early account, that of the divine reward granted to the man who had refused to slay the Saint, and the statement that the shrine had become, by Bede's own day, a place of healing.

> The soldier who had been moved by divine intuition to refuse to slay God's confessor was beheaded at the same time as Alban. And although he had not received a purification of baptism, there was no doubt that he was cleansed by the shedding of his own blood, and rendered fit to enter the Kingdom of Heaven. Astonished by these many strange miracles, the Judge called a halt to the persecution, and whereas he had formerly fought to crush devotion to Christ, he now began to honour the death of his saints.
>
> St Alban suffered on the twenty-second day of June near the city of Verulamium, which the English now call Verlamacaestir. Here, when the peace of Christian times was restored, a beautiful church worthy of his martyrdom was built, where sick folk are healed and frequent miracles take place to this day.

Thus was laid the foundation of the great cult which was to arise in Alban's name and of the mighty structure which was to stand on the hill where he suffered.

The building to be seen there now is by no means the first on the site. Churches erected to honour a saint or other notable Christian figure or event often had humble beginnings. So at St Albans there would most likely be at first a small wooden structure. It was Offa, King of Mercia, who in 793, is said to have vowed to found a monastery on the site after a dream in which were miraculously revealed to him the relics of the Saint. Such an account needs to be treated with caution, having been largely composed by Matthew Paris, a mediaeval historian notable more for imagination than accuracy. Not a great deal is known about the Saxon monastery at St Albans: by comparison with its great Norman successor it was probably quite a primitive place. But it was sacked by the Danes around 870. A church dedicated to St Alban at Odense in Denmark indicates, furthermore, that these fearsome raiders carried off his bones, among much other loot,

'Alban, wearing the priest's long cloak, at once surrendered himself.' (Arrest of St Alban.)

though there are elaborate legends about how they were tricked into taking substitutes while the real ones were for a time kept at Ely.

Verulamium, the Roman *municipium* at the foot of the hill, had long fallen into ruins. The savage invaders who overran the country gradually after the Roman withdrawal, had a superstitious fear of the massive buildings they had left behind, supposing them to have been the work of giants. They certainly never lived among them, preferring to keep their distance, using them, when necessary, as convenient stone quarries. This happened at St Albans, whose Saxon abbots also exerted their authority in routing out the brigands and other undesirables who were using the ruins of Verulamium as sinister hiding-places.

Thus, where Alban had once known the life of a Roman gentleman, and walked in the forum, and along the straight streets of an ordered civilisation, barbarism had taken over, just as might happen after a nuclear strike nowadays. The survivor was the faith to which he had so notably contributed.

The great days of St Albans Abbey really began with the coming of the Normans. Lanfranc, Archbishop of Canterbury, in the course of his vigorous reconstituting of the English monastic houses, in 1107 appointed his cousin, Paul de Caen, as abbot. Under his drive the old Saxon buildings, by that time in a bad state, were largely demolished, so that once again the ruins of Verulamium were pillaged for stone and Roman brick and the beginnings of the great building we see today were made. Life changed also for the monks. The rule of St Benedict was firmly enforced. By 1115, which saw the consecration of the Norman abbey, it had a scriptorium, or library and book-copying centre among the most notable in the whole country. It also had wealth, from lands and bequests: it had convents or cells – in other words, satellite houses – in places as distant as Tynemouth, Wallingford, Wymondham in Norfolk and elsewhere. It had also a monastic school, metamorphosed over many centuries into the St Albans School of today which occupies, among much else, the fourteenth-century gatehouse, the sole remaining part of the once very extensive monastic building.

All of which brings us back to Nicholas Breakspear, whose father's grave, as I saw when I arrived, had just been uncovered by the new excavations. Under this English Pope, Adrian IV, the abbey benefited much, he having been a native of St Albans, although refused entry as a novice. So it was Adrian who, among other things, freed the abbey from the jurisdiction, financial and otherwise, of the Bishop of Lincoln. Released from all episcopal authority other than that of the Pope himself, St Albans became a place of vast importance.

The first draft of Magna Carta was read there in 1213, the then Abbot, John de Cella, having been involved with the barons in their quarrel with King John. There were constant traffickings with the papacy. There were royal favours. Edward I stayed at the monastery seven times. Queen Eleanor's body, after she had died in the North, being brought back to Westminster in stages, rested at St Albans before the high altar. There were triumphs, such as the reputation achieved by the abbey as a centre for art and historical writings. One of its monks, John Walsingham, was a major historian of fourteenth-century England. There were disasters, as when five bays on the south side of the building collapsed in 1323, or when the Black Death or bubonic plague which in 1349 killed 90 per cent of the surrounding population, took off also forty-seven of the abbey's community of sixty, including the Abbot. There were also great abbots, such as Thomas de la Mere, whose rule of fifty years was a notable time for St Albans. In 1979, at a great service attended by Roman Catholic and Anglican clergy, many of the abbots, whose remains had been uncovered in the excavations under the ancient buildings, were solemnly reinterred.

And always there was the shrine, by the great age of mediaeval pilgrimage one of the most important in England. What did it look like, in all its glory? About 8 feet high, it was carved along its top with scenes from Alban's life, such as the execution already noted, together with the customary supporting caste of angels, kings and ecclesiastics. Square shafts surrounded it: twisted marble pillars held candles. A wooden lid protected the actual relics in their bier atop the main structure. This has vanished, but the hole may still be seen, above which hung the rope by which the wooden protective lid could be raised and lowered. Royal gifts of treasures and jewels surrounded the bier. There was also a large Roman cameo, quite possibly discovered at some time or other among the ruins of Verulamium. This was held to be of much value to women in childbirth, and would be taken to them to afford relief. A silver bowl hung before the shrine to receive pilgrims' alms. A short 'life' of Alban, in English, was exhibited for the benefit of those who could read. There was also a painting of Alban.

11

The Shrine of St Alban. Broken up at the time of the Dissolution of the Monasteries, its many scattered portions were brought together in this reconstruction. The casket containing the relics would have stood on the top of the shrine. Behind can be seen the Watchers Loft, where monks kept guard over the treasures of the shrine. (*Cathedral and Abbey Church of St Alban*)

All this was, of course, swept away eventually. The end came actually in December 1539; but long before, decay had set in for the same reasons and by the same means as we noted earlier. The Abbot and such monks as remained were pensioned off, just as elsewhere at this time. The Crown took the treasures from the shrine: books from the famous library went to those of Oxford or Cambridge universities and elsewhere, which may account for the *Life of Alban* by Matthew Paris being at Trinity College, Dublin. Finally, the great monastic buildings were left to decay, or to be pulled down by a certain Sir Richard Lee, one of the friends to whom Henry VIII gave the right to do with them as he wished. He built a mansion for himself with some of the stone.

There followed 300 years of obscurity for the abbey. Time ticked slowly away in the great decaying building, but in the

1870s a great restoration was begun, as in other places about the same time. The results of this were not always happy; great buildings could fall into the hands of enthusiastic magnates who sometimes, in the high noon of Victorian wealth, had more money than discretion. Such a one was Edmund Beckett, later Lord Grimthorpe, a railway magnate and millionaire whose wealth, lavishly given at the price of having his own way as to the manner in which it was done, restored much of St Albans Abbey, which also about this time became the cathedral of a new diocese. So the marks of Lord Grimthorpe are everywhere; but nowhere more remarkably so than in the West porch, a place where today's pilgrim may well take his leave of this fascinating place. There is there a winged representation of St Matthew. But there is something strange about the features. Well there may be, for they are those of Lord Grimthorpe himself.

When I was there on that sunny day I found it very rewarding, as a farewell to St Albans, to walk down the hill up which, so long, long ago, Alban had gone to his death. He could never have known how, by that act of heroism, inspired by something in the faith and personality of the fugitive he had sheltered, so great an oak was to grow from so small an acorn. But nowadays, to look up from the park which now covers Roman Verulamium, and to see across the River Ver, above the trees today's great cathedral, throbbing with life and people, worthy successors to yesterday's pilgrims, is to realise that this is in fact where pilgrim's England began.

The cathedral of the Fens

To me, Ely Cathedral is a very strange place and always will be. I have visited it many times in summer and winter, and slept in some of the canons' houses around, which together make one of the most notable collections of mediaeval houses still inhabited. Its strangeness for me never diminishes. Once when I was there it was winter, and a raw wind blowing out of Russia – there is scarcely a sizeable hill between this place and the Urals – was moaning in the great Lantern Tower. The organist, although it was after nine at night, was practising, so that the booming of the great organ came eerily out of the darkness of the vast building. Everything is on a huge scale here, so huge that it often seems

Ely Cathedral from the South. The great Octagon and Lantern Tower, one of the great engineering achievements of the Middle Ages, can be seen on the right. (*The British Tourist Authority*)

empty, except for its ghosts, however many visitors there may be around the place. There is a tradition that Augustine was the founder of the first church. But the Ely story really begins with the founding of a convent on this Isle of Ely in 673 by Etheldreda, daughter of Anna, a Christian king of the East Angles, a kingdom covering roughly the area of the present Norfolk and Suffolk. Born at Exning near Newmarket, Etheldreda in the fullness of time became this convent's first Abbess.

A convent now means a community of women religious. In Etheldreda's time it betokened a community of both men and women – a double monastery. The word 'abbess' signified the superiority of such a place. Saxon culture, in this respect very different from Norman, seemed to find no difficulty in accepting feminine leadership of this sort. An abbess in such times would usually be of noble, or preferably royal, blood. But, whatever advantages of birth she might have, she would certainly require to be a strong personality. Etheldreda, like another notable abbess of Saxon times, Hilda of Whitby, was clearly a remarkable woman.

But at the same time, being a woman, she was, in the years before taking the veil, subject to marriage. The difficulty here lay in the matter of virginity. From the earliest times, and for reasons too complex to be entered upon here, there has existed a close connection between virginity and sanctity. Thus, it is a part of Etheldreda's story to note how the chroniclers of it make much of the report that, in spite of marriage, she retained her virginity, although married twice. After the death of her first husband, Tondbert, a prince of the fenmen, she withdrew to this Isle of Ely in order to devote herself to a life of prayer, with a selected group of her ladies. Five years later she was pressed, for reasons of state, to marry Egfrith, son of Oswy, King of Northumbria. This marriage likewise was not consummated. A vivid illustration of the difficulty of maintaining this state of affairs is to be found in a sculpture on one of the corbels in the octagon of Ely Cathedral, which present in eight episodes incidents from the life of Etheldreda. This one shows the Saint, pursued by her second husband, from whom she had fled, in refuge with her attendant women on the promontory of St Abbs' Head. Stormy seas and high tides, miraculously continued for days, kept him away from her, subsiding only when he had withdrawn. Twelve years after this marriage Egfrith let her go to become a nun after all that time as a princess in Northumbria.

'Stormy seas and high tides, miraculously continued for days, kept him away
from her. . . .' (St Etheldreda pursued by her husband on St Abb's Head.)

It must have been a strangely divided life. In private, and by conviction, she was a religious: in public she would always have been required to appear at her husband's side – he was sixteen at their marriage, she thirty – in the rough Court of the times, sitting at high table with him in the evenings when the log fire was lit and the drink went round, and stories of the wild and fierce events of the day would be exchanged. This is not to say that Anglo-Saxon civilisation of this kind was necessarily savage; but it was certainly rough. So we can imagine Etheldreda in these days as a Saxon lady presiding in such company. She would by habit wear much rich jewellery around her neck, as was the custom of the times for persons of her rank. We shall hear more of this matter later. Meanwhile Etheldreda found in Northumbria a life in one respect to her taste. The kingdom, through the efforts partly of Celtic missionaries, was a land where Christianity was firmly established when she arrived there. The great spiritual influence of St Aidan, and his successor St Finan, Bishop of Lindisfarne, carried on his work. However, Etheldreda received the veil from St Wilfrid in 672 at Coldingham in the North, where her aunt was abbess. A year later, after a long and wearisome journey with a handful of her women, she arrived on the Isle of Ely, which territory had come to her through her first marriage to Tondbert. And there she founded the double monastery.

Bede has a good deal to say about Etheldreda, some of it very curious, such as that she would never wash in warm water except on the eve of the greater festivals, or always wore wool, never linen next to the skin. She would only eat one meal a day, and always remained at prayer in the church from the hour of matins, which would be just after midnight, until dawn. He claims for her many other austerities and other gifts, including that of prophecy. After a reign of seven years she died, and from her death and subsequent events sprang her reputation for sanctity and the growth of her cult.

She was buried in a wooden coffin like any other nun, at her own request. But her sister Sexburga, who succeeded her as abbess, decided to have the remains exhumed, placed in a stone coffin and transferred into the church. But where was a stone coffin to be found? Certainly not in the Fens around Ely where, as Bede quaintly says, there were 'no large stones'. Some of the brethren were therefore sent by boat to find something suitable. So they set off by boat and, in 'a small ruined city not far distant which the English call Grantchester' they discovered a complete

Scenes from the life of St Etheldreda, once in Ely Cathedral. At the top left she is being married to Egfrith. On the right she is leaving him in order to return to the monastic life in Coldingham. At the bottom left she is shown building the monastery at Ely. The bottom right shows her body being moved to the monastery in 695 from its original burial place. (*Society of Antiquaries of London*)

sarcophagus. At one time, by legend, this was supposed to be of marble; but when the shrine was dismantled at the Reformation it was found to be of stone. Even so, it was obviously of Roman origin, for Grantchester as its name implies, had been a Roman settlement. The strange probability therefore arises that the remains of Etheldreda came to rest in a tomb once

19

occupied by the corpse of some Roman notable of long ago.

When her body was transferred from its wooden coffin it was found to be miraculously preserved, a fact which Bede ascribes to the fact that she 'had remained untainted by bodily intercourse'. The scene of the transference of her body to the sarcophagus which later came to be the focus of her shrine is depicted in a fifteenth-century panel, now the property of the Society of Antiquaries, found by chance being used as a cupboard door in a house in Ely. It had probably at one time been an altarpiece, and shows also her marriage to Egfrith, her retirement to a convent and the building of her church at Ely.

The origin of the cult of Etheldreda, and especially of the healing powers ascribed to her relics, takes us back to that matter of the long Saxon necklaces which, as a princess, she was wont to wear. Her final illness, which caused her much suffering and probably arose in the course of some local pestilence, took the form of a large tumour below her jaw. 'A burning red tumour', she is said to have described it, 'instead of gold and pearls', which she saw as a punishment inflicted upon her for those former vanities of the flesh. This tumour features in Bede's account of the transference of her body to the sarcophagus. A physician named Cynifrid who had attended her during her last illness was also present at the exhumation and testified that:

> I was asked to open the tumour and drain away the poisonous matter in it. I did this, and for two days she seemed somewhat easier, so that many thought that she would recover from her illness. But on the third day her earlier pain returned, and she was taken this world, and exchanged all pain and death for everlasting life and health. When her bones were to be taken up out of the grave so many years later, a pavilion was raised over it, and the whole community stood around it chanting, the brothers on one side, and the sisters on the other.
>
> The Abbess herself, with a few others, went in to take up and wash the bones, when we suddenly heard her cry out in loud voice: 'Glory to the name of the Lord!'. Shortly afterwards they opened the door of the pavilion and called me in. There I saw the body of the Holy Virgin taken from its grave and laid on a bed as though asleep; and when they had uncovered her face, they showed me that the incision which I had made had healed.

This took place in 695. When, centuries later, there were, as there still are, two annual St Audrey's fairs held at Ely on 23 June and 17 October, cheap 'tawdry lace' would be sold. From this has come the word 'tawdry', an adjective denoting something showy but worthless, of excessive or tasteless finery. Surely few words in current use can have had a more curious origin. Bede claims very powerful curative properties from the relics of Etheldreda, such as that devils could be expelled from the bodies of sufferers by the touch of robes she had worn. Her original wooden coffin was held to have been especially effective in treating diseases of the eye, provided patients placed their heads on it as they prayed.

In 870 a terrible calamity came upon the Saxon religious house which Etheldreda had founded when it was totally destroyed by a raiding Danish army. Two centuries of peaceful life had followed under a succession of abbesses after Etheldreda's time and then this Danish army came burning and looting. They destroyed Ely, Peterborough and other religious houses, murdering most of the inmates, men and women or, as was quite customary, burning them alive in their own buildings. A chronicle of the time states that 'the monastery which Etheldreda the true servant of Christ had founded was burnt, together with the nuns, the ornaments and relics of the saints, and the city was set on fire and looted. Everything that could be carried away was taken by the enemies of God.' For a century after this frightful event little stirred among the ruins, until the great monastic revival led by St Dunstan and St Oswald.

With the support of King Edgar the Peaceful, a new community this time of men only, was gathered together under Abbot Brithnoth and rebuilding was begun in 970. The *Anglo-Saxon Chronicle* makes it clear that this building was quite considerable. And in it was not only a splendid image of the Virgin but also, still intact, the relics of Etheldreda. These, according to the *Liber Eliensis*, 'lay splendidly entombed in a tower on the south side of the High Altar and her glorious sister Sexburga shone honourably entombed in the same place on the north side'. Indeed, there were more. In this rebuilt church there were the shrines of Etheldreda, of her sister Sexburga, of her daughter St Ermelinda and St Werburga, her daughter. The fact that a third sister, Withberga, who had founded an abbey at East Dereham in Norfolk, had been enshrined in the church there, led the Abbot and monks of Ely to feel very strongly that her body should be brought to join the others of her family at Ely. In the event they stole it by a ruse. The Abbot arranged a feast in the manor at Dereham, which had been given by King Edgar to Ely Monastery, in 974. While the feasting was in progress, the Ely monks 'contrived to steal the body of Withberga out of the church, and to drive away with it in a cart to Brendon, where they placed it in a boat which was waiting in readiness to take it to Ely'. It is not a very edifying story; but it is some reflection upon the great value attached to relics at the time.

An even less edifying tale, also involving the monks of Ely, involves no less a person than St Alban. This was a notable scandal. Fearing a Danish raid, the monks of St Albans entrusted the bodies of their saint to Ely for safe keeping. However, in order to make doubly sure that the remains of St Alban would in fact be kept safe, they placed an anonymous skeleton in the casket sent to Ely, while hiding the real remains near by. When, the particular menace having passed, the time came for the Ely monks to return the casket, they removed what they thought were the real Saint's relics and in their turn substituted them by worthless bones. Leofric, Abbot of St Albans, had marked his particular false bones and therefore detected the fraud. Eventually, a full investigation was held and, according to the historian Matthew Paris, monk of St Albans, the verdict went in favour of St Albans.

But it was the Normans who created the vast and astonishing building which is the present Ely Cathedral. The old Saxon building was entirely swept away. Ovin's cross in the south aisle of the nave is the only remaining Saxon relic. The monk Ovin was Etheldreda's steward and trusted minister. His cross, which has lost its top, was found by a historian of Ely, James Bentham, in the eighteenth century, being used as a mounting post in the village of Haddenham near by and was brought back by him into the cathedral. It has a moving inscription in Latin which, translated, says 'Grant oh God to Ovin thy light and rest'. Ovin's cross, being the oldest monument in Ely Cathedral, is a good place from which to begin an exploration of the mighty building around.

It is striking that the Normans, conquerors as they were, yet continued without question the veneration of a saint who belonged to the tradition of a now subject race. Although Etheldreda had been a Saxon queen, her sanctity overrode considerations of race and history. So at Ely, as elsewhere, they set about the creation of a building in honour of God and his saint more splendid by far than any which had stood there before.

Why did they create these vast structures at all? This is not, of course, a question peculiar to Ely. It is raised by any ancient cathedral. Obviously, such places reflected the wealth and ambitions of the communities creating, maintaining and, where possible, increasing them. To that extent they were status symbols, often highly competitive one with another. Equally obviously they represented the popularity of the pilgrim cult which was a major source of income. And yet, behind and beyond these worldly considerations, there was always another motive, that of giving glory to God by erecting in his name a building which, by reaching up into the very heavens, could inspire the human spirit to do the same.

This is not an easy matter to comprehend. It represents a completely different outlook from ours which, by habit, looks at everything from the manward end, considering always how this or that serves some human purpose. When I was a canon of an ancient cathedral one question often asked by visitors was where did the congregation of such a place come from? These visitors would be looking at the great nave, with its soaring pillars and vaulted roof, and space enough to accommodate possibly 1,000 people. The answer, that there was no congregation when such places were built, was clearly puzzling. Yet such is the fact. A great cathedral such as Ely, or any other like it, was not created for people at all. The community would worship in their choir, their voices a mutter in the surrounding vastness. That belonged to God. Outside, in the town of narrow streets and huddled buildings was a different world altogether. Any mediaeval cathedral, in its original setting, would have looked like some vision of Heaven, and be equally difficult to get into as well.

Questions are often asked as to how such places were built. It is a good question. It needs to be remembered, with awed respect, when looking at such a place as Ely Cathedral, that its builders had no power machinery at their disposal whatever. What is more, their materials, including thousands of tons of stone and timber, had to be transported to the site over a roadless land, frequently deep in mud and much of it forest or wilderness. In the case of Ely the surroundings were actually water. Furthermore, the tools available were rudimentary, all scaffolding needed to be of timber lashed together. How these difficulties were overcome can be illustrated by what in fact happened at Ely. And since that building, with its unique Lantern Tower, exhibits one of the greatest engineering feats of mediaeval building in Britain and possibly in Europe, it is as good a place as any to find a further answer to this question.

To stand in the Early English Galilee porch, the western entrance to the cathedral, and to look down the nave stretching away eastwards between Norman columns each 72 feet high to the roof, with an exceptionally high clerestory, is to get some idea of the huge scale of the place. Actually, the Norman building was commenced at the eastern end in the time of Abbot Simeon, a man appointed by the Conqueror at the exceptional age of eighty-six. But he was vigorous enough to regain much of the monastic property which had been dispersed at the Conquest, and to begin a cruciform church with an absidal east end. There were many interruptions to the work in succeeding years and under succeeding abbots, some of them serious and prolonged interruptions. William's successor, for instance, appropriated to his own use the income of the abbacy so that work ceased until 1100, when it was recommenced under a new abbot, Richard of Bec.

Yet building went on, moving steadily westwards. By 1106 there was enough completed to make it possible for the body of St Etheldreda, placed so long ago in the Roman sarcophagus discovered at Grantchester, to be moved – 'translated' was the word normally used – into a shrine eastward of the high altar. Finally, the church which had been begun under Abbot Simeon was completed in 1189. It was already by then an architectural masterpiece, as it still is, a fit place for any pilgrim to marvel at.

One important matter facilitated its construction in that a supply of stone of exceptional quality was to be had in a quarry at Barnack near Stamford. So Ely is built largely of this Barnack stone, carried there, as might have been expected, along waterways on barges, or 'keels' as they were called. There were other stones used, and other sources drawn upon, as can be seen easily enough by looking around; but this was the chief. Skilled labour came from the specialists, master masons and master carpenters, glaziers and sculptors, who would be known by reputation and called in to create works which often took years to complete. These mediaeval architects were the key men of buildings of the age. For that reason it is incorrect to speak of this or that cleric 'building a church' or part of one. Bishop Eustace of Ely from 1197 to 1215 is said, for example, to have built the beautiful Galilee porch. What this really means is that he caused it to be done. But the design and the actual work lay in the hands of master craftsmen and their men. Sometimes their names have been preserved; but often they are forgotten. A particularly splendid example of their work in Ely is the sculpture above the porch over the prior's door.

Two further events went into the making of the present Ely Cathedral. One, the extension of the church eastwards in the time of Bishop Hugh de Northwold in the thirteenth century was due to the increasing popularity of the cult of Etheldreda. This was the origin of the Six Bay Presbytery to which, in a ceremony of great splendour, and in the presence of King Henry III and his son, the relics of the Saint and her sisters were moved in a third and last 'translation', the whole church being rededicated at the same time to St Etheldreda, St Mary and St Peter. This was on an October day in 1252.

Thus it remained for seventy years, the goal of thousands of pilgrims making their way across the Fens from far and wide to the famous shrine. And then, on 12 February 1322 an enormous catastrophe took place. The great central tower, with a rumble and a roar and a cascade of masonry, collapsed.

Such happenings were not unknown. Mediaeval builders, like their modern counterparts, made their mistakes, or were overcome by problems unforeseen. What matters is the truly astonishing manner in which the disaster at Ely was turned into an architectural triumph, leading to the creation of the octagon, with the timber roof and lantern above it.

At this time of supreme challenge some of the craftsmen who were called upon to cope with it emerged from the usual anonymity in which the years have buried them. Thus the Ely Sacrist Rolls refer to Master Thomas, carpenter, sent for to set up a great crane: to a mason, Master John, to an adviser on the work, Peter Quadratarius, to another master carpenter, William Hurley. He was already distinguished in his profession, being Surveyor of all the royal works of carpentry at the Tower of London. Ely paid him £8 a year, a large fee by the standards of the time. Among the clerical body were also persons of ability: John of Hotham, Bishop: John Crauden, Prior. But the key man was undoubtedly the then Sacristan, Alan of Walsingham: 'A man in every way qualified for that station, especially as, among his other accomplishments, he was eminently skilful in architecture and in other mechanical arts.' He must have been, to originate the huge engineering marvel which became the octagon. His head is carved on one of the arches around this octagon; but his real memorial is the amazing creation which soars above. The essence of it is that he did not rebuild this tower but replaced it by something quite different. On top of the pillars surrounding the octagon, which stonework itself required years to complete, were set vertically eight corner posts, each a complete oak, each 70 feet long, each weighing around 10 tons. The Sacrist Rolls contain the statement that in 1322 'Alan the Sacristan Master, Thomas the carpenter' went to Chicksand in Bedfordshire and bought twenty oak trees for £9. How these were got to Ely, above all how, when prepared, they were hauled up to stand vertically upon their stone bases 100 feet up above the floor of the cathedral is a mystery. On top of them and supported by them, amid intricate timber work, was the lantern and roof weighing, with its wood and lead, some 400 tons. There it has stood through the centuries; defying time, neglect and weather, glorified by painting and glass and crowned with a life-size carving of Christ in Glory looking down 150 feet. Today's pilgrim, approaching Ely, sees this lantern as the main feature of the great building. Inside, however, he will find no mediaeval shrine to St Etheldreda. That went the way of all the rest at the Reformation, and what remains of her bones lie buried beneath the tomb of Bishop Hotham. The destruction of images and of what must have been splendid sculptures, particularly to be noticed in the Lady chapel, took place around this time. But the lasting memorial to the Saxon Queen to whose shrine so many for so long made their way is this astonishing building which arose around her cult and which still bears witness to the faith which, as always, survives time and chance.

CHAPTER 2

Across East Anglia

Norwich – St William and Mother Julian
Bromholm – The vanished shrine of the Holy Rood
Walsingham – The House of the Holy Family
King's Lynn – Margery Kempe

Norwich and the strange tale of St William

Norwich is a fine city, as the notice placed alongside the main approaches to it states. It stands in the centre of East Anglia, and to pass from Ely, gaunt in its fenland isolation, to this bustling place, is to enter another world.

If ever there was a land of pilgrims, and shrines, and mediaeval cults of saints local and national, this is it. The land was crossed and recrossed by their tracks. They came at it from all sides, some by sea to land at Bromholm on the north-east coast to visit the Holy Rood; others at Lynn on the opposite coast to make their way to Walsingham. There is a Palmers Way which united near Newmarket many routes to that famous shrine. Always this part of England was special and distinct. There was a particular reason for this: Norwich was not only one of the great cities of the Middle Ages: it was also the most isolated. The Fens to the west, and the sea on three sides saw to that. So it lived its own life and, in a way, still does. Not surprisingly, therefore, it had numerous local saints, almost unknown anywhere else. There was a portion of the blood of the Virgin in the Cathedral Priory at Norwich, part of the shirt of St Edmund, King and Martyr in St Edmund's Church there, John the Baptist's head in a place called Trimingham, a famous image of the Virgin at Thetford and so on.

But it is in Norwich Cathedral that the site of one of the

Norwich Cathedral from the castle. The spire, 315 feet, is the second highest in England. The cathedral, which became the centre of a great Benedictine Monastery, was begun by the Normans in 1096, using stone brought from Caen. The cult of the boy saint, William of Norwich, probably owed something to the need of the cathedral to have the one thing it lacked – a saint of its own. (*A. F. Kersting*)

strangest and saddest and, in its consequence grimmest, of all popular cults is to be found. In the Jesus Chapel, an unremarkable spot now in a great building which contains so many treasures, was this shrine of St William, a boy said to have been the victim of Jewish ritual murder. It was the first such legend of any note. It began what was to become a recurring theme in anti-Semitism. The story of Little St Hugh of Lincoln is almost a mirror-image of it, and the fanatical anti-Jew propaganda of Nazi Germany in this century perpetuated it in various forms. As to what happened, the *Anglo-Saxon Chronicle* states that: 'The Jews of Norwich bought a Christian child before Easter and tortured him with all the torture that our Lord was tortured with; and on Good Friday hanged him on a cross on account of our Lord, and then buried him.' There is a very unusual painting of this 'crucifixion' on the screen in Loddon Church, some 12 miles south-east of Norwich.

These alleged events took place in Holy Week of 1144. On the Monday of that week the boy William, a twelve-year-old apprentice leather worker, was lured away from home by someone offering him better employment. On the following Saturday a party of so-called Jews were surprised with a body, tied up on horseback like a sack. When questioned they fled, and the body was buried on the spot. A small chapel marks that place still. But the body was not left long undisturbed. The boy's relatives began rumours, such as that William had been seen entering a house of the Jewish quarter just before his disappearance. This might have been true, for the boy had made friends among the wealthy Hebrews who lived, under royal protection, near Norwich Castle. The city, then the third wealthiest in England, needed these 'King's Jews' as traders and moneylenders, since they alone were permitted to practise the usury forbidden by Church law to Christians. But there was a strong undercurrent of dislike of them and of their wealth. When, therefore, what the family was saying spread around, the citizens echoed it. His uncle accused the terrified Jews to a church synod in Norwich. The idea of martyrdom gathered in strength. The body was exhumed and reburied in a monks' cemetery. Finally a certain Thomas of Monmouth, becoming a monk at Norwich in 1150, took up the cause of William, convinced he was a saint and martyr, and also, quite probably, moved by the consideration that the cathedral would benefit by having a saint which up to that time it lacked. It was he who caused the second burial-place

Martyrdom of the boy saint William of Norwich. A rare picture from the altar piece of Loddon Church, Norfolk, shows the popular belief that the Jews of Norwich first tortured and then sacrificed him on Good Friday 1144. (*Anglia Television*)

of William to be reopened. The little skeleton was wrapped in linens and buried this time in the chapter-house, but so many pilgrims visited it there that a further 'translation' became necessary, this time to a martyrs' chapel, now the Jesus chapel. Eventually the boy was canonised and Thomas of Monmouth compiled a book called *The Life and Miracles of St William*.

Many miracles took place around the shrine, which is a most extraordinary fact in an extraordinary story. Thomas of Monmouth recorded them over a period of twenty years. Most seem to have been of local people; but some came from further afield. A man from York was said to have struggled all the way from that city to the shrine, and being cured by St William, left his crutches there as a sign of the fact. There was a soldier from Lorraine who, having been sent by the Pope on a penitential journey for burning a church, found that the iron bands which had been affixed to his arms, broke off at the tomb of the boy saint. Other fantastic cures were recorded. The blind saw, the lame walked, the demented became sane. Few other mediaeval cults drew so many pilgrims from the immediate locality, both from the merchant and artisan classes, and from the lower clergy, significant facts in that both groups were prone to anti-Semitism. The merchants would be jealous of the Jewish wealth, the more ignorant clergy would be convinced of Jewish implication in the death of Christ.

It is a strange tale. How the boy died has never been discovered. It certainly cannot have been a Jewish act, being completely alien to their faith and practice. But it brought cruel retribution upon them. William, in the end, was famous not for his merits – he hardly existed until he had died – but because the Jews were said to have murdered him. As to why so many cures were performed at William's shrine, it is impossible to give any answer except to say that the whole thing belongs to the strange wonder world of mediaeval saints, where, given enough people disposed to belief, anything could happen – and did.

Mother Julian the mystic

In another part of this fascinating city there is the reminder both of a notable woman of Norwich and of an important feature of the mediaeval pilgrim world. This is the cell of the mystic, the Lady Julian. She was an anchoress, the female equivalent of an anchorite, of whom many could be found living lives of almost total seclusion in some 'hold' or cell, usually attached to a particular church. There were probably as many as fifty at various times in Norwich in the Middle Ages. Such people differed from the hermit, who also sought seclusion, by the fact that whereas he could move about at will, the anchorite or anchoress was under ecclesiastical authority and could go about, if at all, only by permission. A celebrated work, *The Ancren Riwle*, was the manual generally used for the regulation of their conduct. Indulgences were granted to pilgrims who visited them.

The Lady Julian was a distinguished member of that strange body of people, and pilgrims certainly sought her out, for there is a map in the cathedral indicating the route from there to her cell, which once contained a little window looking out on the street at which the anchoress could give spiritual counsel. Margery Kempe, a mystic of a very different type, visited her here. A window in the cathedral showing the Lady Julian has a charming addition, the figure of her cat.

Her cell is to be found in the little church of St Julian, in the parish of St Peter, Partmentergate. Because it has been restored and is maintained by a religious community, it is probably the best example to be found anywhere in England of what one of these cells really looked like. It may be found by turning left out of the Erpingham gate of the cathedral, continuing along King Street, and turning right opposite Old Barge Yard. The church is on the left at the junction with Rouen Road. The cell within, where the Lady Julian lived for over forty years, is now furnished as a chapel, contains a shrine and is a place of pilgrimage for people from the world over. A rack full of notes left by visitors asking Mother Julian for help is a testimony to the reality of her continuing influence. There was a room next door for a servant, of whom Julian had two in her lifetime: Sara and Alice. There is a lovely silence in this cell, a place lived in by other solitaries before and after Julian.

She was born in 1342. On 8 May 1373, during severe illness, she received sixteen 'shewings', or visions of Christ. For twenty years she meditated upon them, and at length recorded their meaning in her famous *Revelations of Divine Love*, acknowledged as one of the great classics of spiritual literature. It was also, incidentally, the first known book written by an Englishwoman. There are excerpts from it framed on the walls of her cell now, including the famous: 'All shall be well, and all manner of things shall be well', words which have meant much to many in suffering and adversity over the centuries. Julian lived, as we do, in times of great anxieties and fearful happenings. We have the nuclear threat, among other terrors; she had the Black Death, the Peasants' Revolt, wars with France, and years of national disturbance, all of which were felt in Norwich itself.

These outward events give extra significance to her deeply experienced discovery that God who made this world was all loving, and that his ultimate purpose was loving. The

A highly stylish representation of the celebrated mystic, Mother Julian of Norwich, whose 14th century Revelation of Divine Love are a spiritual classic. At her feet is her pet cat. Her cell or dwelling place, in a street near the cathedral, was visited by pilgrims, and still is. (*Norfolk County Library*)

contemporary significance of her work is striking. The famous picture of our earth taken from a spacecraft *en route* to the moon, for example, is curiously reflected in her vision of God showing her 'a little thing, the size of a hazel-nut, on the palm of my hand, round like a ball. I looked at it thoughtfully and wondered "What is this?" And the answer came: "It is all that is made." I marvelled that it continued to exist. . . . It was so small. . . .'

A cathedral full of light

Norwich Cathedral, with its spire, at 315 feet, the second highest in England after Salisbury, is a very wonderful building, and now, as for centuries past, pilgrims converge on it. It is true that Norwich, unlike Ely or St Albans, never had a major saint around which to focus its life. But, as a building, it has in one way benefited from this. No space has ever had to be made before or behind the high altar to accommodate a shrine. So there has been preserved in Norwich a feature unique to any English cathedral, a bishop's throne, the stones of which date from the eighth century, behind the altar. This is still used, and its like, which reaches back to the very earliest days of the Christian Church, when worship was conducted in public buildings or in larger houses, can be found nowhere else, although there are unused survivals at Hexham and Beverley.

But this is only one of the treasures of this famous building. For me, the contrast between Norwich and Ely is that between darkness and light. Ely is a sombre place; Norwich seems full of light. It is built of Caen stone, light coloured in itself, which was brought by sea from Normandy, then up the river to Norwich and to the cathedral site by a specially cut canal. It seems to glisten, as one recent dean put it, in the clear East Anglian sunshine, and the three tiers of windows; clerestory, triforium and nave give a sense of transcendence. Pilgrims used to process through the ambulatory around the high altar. They would have visited the reliquary chapel, now gone; and marvelled at the reliquary arch, built about 1424 to house relics. And of course, during the time of his cult, they would have gone to the shrine of Little St William. Norwich is very much a Norman creation, built at the same time as the castle. Its founder was Herbert de Losinga, who came to Norwich first from Ramsey in

Huntingdonshire where he had been abbot, and then from Thetford where he had been appointed bishop by William Rufus in 1091. He had been educated at Fécamp and, in spite of his name, was probably a native of Suffolk, all of which details have a relevance in showing that, whatever his ultimate origins, he was a Norman by training and predilection. It was he who brought the Benedictine Order, with its discipline and rule, to Norwich, and it was certainly he who pushed through the creation of the cathedral with singular vigour and determination. The foundation stone was laid in 1096, the first consecration took place in the September of 1101, which is an astonishing record, especially in view of the fact that at the same time the same man was engaged in the building of the great priory parish churches of St Nicholas Yarmouth and St Margaret's at Lynn. De Losinga died in 1119 and was buried before the high altar where his grave slab is still to be seen. It was at the enthronement of his successor Everard de Montgomery in 1121 that the ancient throne was probably brought from Thetford and placed in the position which it now uniquely occupies.

Norwich Cathedral Priory, as it came to be called, was a very large establishment and, because its life and organisation are recorded in unusual detail in the still extant Rolls of Norwich Cathedral Priory, it is possible to gather from this source something of what the real life of such an establishment must have been right through the Middle Ages, from the twelfth century to the Dissolution in the sixteenth. So, for many years, there would be some sixty monks in residence. There would be hospitality given to rich and poor: there would be the daily round of services which formed the Opus Dei, or Work of God, which was the main duty of the monastic body. But it is some of the curious details available from the Rolls which fill out the picture in a most interesting way. There was a master of the cellar, responsible for the entertainment of guests, with a staff of fifty. There is an authentic touch in the information that, on his staff, he had a curer of herrings, which no doubt were brought up from Yarmouth. Ten thousand eggs a week were consumed by this community and its large number of ancillary workers. Then there was the Sacrist, responsible, as a sacrist still is, for the furnishings of worship. But this one used 11 hundredweight of wool every year and bought cloth from as far afield as Antioch. The Precentor cared for the music and its books. The Chamberlain arranged the clothing of the establishment. The Almoner was responsible for giving to the poor, of which, as throughout the Middle Ages there were many: lepers, beggars, vagrants and the like. Further, the Hosteler looked after the guest hall: the Refectorer was responsible for the dining hall: the Infirmar for the infirmary. So there existed in Norwich a very large and important monastic community.

Norwich Cathedral is a treasure-house of the past which is all the more delightful in that it is quite clearly a treasure-house of the present as well, because it bears every mark of being loved and cared for and used. Whenever I go there, which is often, I always like to contemplate it from outside as well as in because only by so doing is it possible to see the truly marvellous impressiveness of the whole building, and to wonder at and to be thankful for the calamities which it has so triumphantly survived.

The Holy Rood of Bromholm

For me, the journey from Norwich, northwards along the B1150 to North Walsham, and thence some 5 miles to the coast at Bacton, has a peculiar fascination, based upon the very curious story of Bromholm Priory, the ruins of which – a gatehouse, a transept, a perfect line of stone arches – loom up at the approach to Bacton itself. It is, at any rate in March, a bleak enough part of the world: the brown sea crashes at high tide against the breakwaters; little chalets by the sea are shuttered, waiting for summer; and between Bromholm and that sea are empty fields and three huge empty churches with pale East Anglian light emphasising the flinty greyness of their walls. Yet this was once a very notable place of pilgrimage indeed. It was even for a time as well known as Canterbury. The Paston family, of the famous *Paston Letters*, lived near by and were patrons of it. The Holy Rood: 'Two transverse pieces of wood about the length of a man's hand' is mentioned twice in literature: in the mediaeval poet Langland's *Piers Plowman* and in Chaucer's *Reeves Tale*. From far and near and frequently over the sea, pilgrims thronged the place. Miracles took place there. The chronicler Matthew Paris says that, by its virtues

> dead folk were restored to life, the blind saw, the lame
> walked, lepers were cleansed, those possessed by devils were
> freed; and whosoever might be the sick man who came to the
> Cross with faith in the Holy wood, he departed whole and
> sound. So the aforesaid Cross is frequented, adored and
> worshipped not only by the English nation but also by men of
> far off lands; and those who have heard what divine miracles
> it works most devoutly revere it.

This is why it is so much worth while now to stand in the nettle-strewn solitude of the ruins of Bromholm and think upon what happened.

The story begins with an East Anglian priest who, at the time of the Fourth Crusade in 1204 was chief chaplain and keeper of holy

Ruins of Bromholm Priory, Norfolk, a small Cluniac House which, housing the famous Holy Rood of Bromholm, became a notable pilgrim centre of the Middle Ages. (*Anglia Television*)

relics to Count Baldwin of Flanders. When the crusaders sacked and pillaged Constantinople, the capital of the Christian Empire of the East, this Baldwin became, for a brief time, Emperor. Among his possessions was a small cross believed to have been made from 'the very wood whereon the Saviour of the world hung for the redemption of mankind'. But Baldwin, the first Latin Emperor of the East, was defeated and captured by rebels. His chaplain found himself in possession of this alleged piece of the true Cross, together with various other relics. Accompanied by his two sons, he returned to England and immediately set about trying to dispose of the objects he had brought home with him. At St Albans he managed to sell two fingers of St Margaret and a certain number of jewels; but found no takers for the little cross. So he wandered on, going from monastery to monastery, until finally he came to Bromholm, then a very small and poor Cluniac priory which was a cell of the much greater Cluniac establishment at Castle Acre to the west. There the brethren bought the piece of wood, little knowing what they had set in train by so doing. Thus, there came to this remote corner of north-eastern Norfolk a relic which had belonged to the Greeks, which had been looted by the crusaders, and which had become the accidental possession of this wandering East Anglian priest.

Within an astonishingly short space of time, the Holy Rood at Bromholm became celebrated as a pilgrim shrine. In 1226 Henry III visited the place, at the same time granting the priory the right to hold a fair of three days for the Festival of Exaltation of the Cross on 14 September. From this, and the further right to hold a fair on the Feast of St Andrew on 30 November, came much of the income of the priory. There were, from time to time, notable gifts such as an image of himself presented by Henry III, and a grant of land from Edward II, and from Henry V, in 1416, 'four pipes of wine annually from the ports of Yarmouth and Kirkby'.

Without any doubt at all this Holy Rood, these two pieces of wood once carried in the sleeve of a wandering priest, was genuinely worshipped and was the cause of many miracles experienced by pilgrims to the shrine. To this day there survives in the library at Lambeth Palace an example of the devotional cards which were sold to pilgrims at Bromholm. It shows a cross with two transverse beams and around it the words

This cros yat here peynted is
Signe of ye cros of Bromholm is.

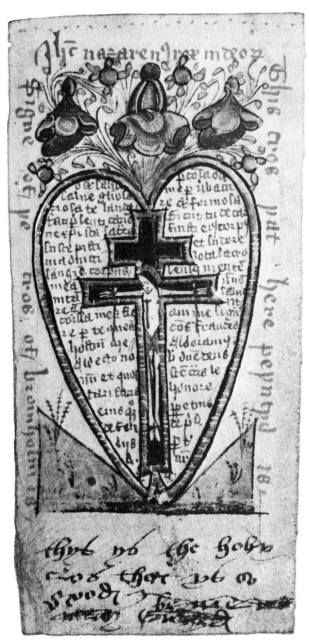

A rare example of one of the 'Prayer Cards' which pilgrims could buy. This came from Bromholm, a once famous shrine of the Holy Rood in north-east Norfolk.
(*His Grace the Archbishop of Canterbury and the Trustees of Lambeth Palace Library*)

But Bromholm, oddly enough, was always a popular rather than an aristocratic centre of pilgrimage, in this way being a marked contrast to the shrine of Our Lady at Walsingham. Herein lies the significance of the two literary mentions of it. *Piers Plowman* was a proletarian poem of protest against the oppressions of the rich: and Chaucer's *Reeves Tale* is a vulgar and extremely funny story told by a working man.

All this, and much more, sprang from the Holy Rood of Bromholm, venerated in a priory represented now only by those haunting ruins on the Norfolk coast. It vanishes from sight in 1537, when one of the agents of Thomas Cromwell wrote to his master saying that he had removed the relic and that it was in his possession. Nothing has been heard of its whereabouts since. It was almost certainly destroyed. But it has been well said of it that 'in the complications of its history, in the tremendous surge of shortlived high fashion followed by three centuries of general popularity it is, perhaps, the most rhapsodical of English centres of pilgrimage. With this quality Bromholm enshrines the full expression of the mediaeval spirit.'

Walsingham, and the House of the Holy Family

The cross-country way from Bromholm to Walsingham, which lies some 5 miles inland from Wells next the Sea, is to return to North Walsham, continue along the B1145 to Aylsham, then to follow the B1364 which leads eventually, after crossing the A148 between Fakenham and Holt, to Walsingham. There are, of course, more obvious ways, but this is my own favourite route, through the deep and quiet country of this remote part of Norfolk.

There have always been many roads to Walsingham, anyway. For there was, as for Roman Catholics there still is, the National Shrine of Our Lady and an Anglican shrine, also. So in the Middle Ages pilgrims found their way there from all directions. The first road mentioned in Holinshed's *English Itinerary* is the route from London to Walsingham, by way of Waltham and Ware. Pilgrims from the North would come by King's Lynn, or Lynn as it was known then. So would people from overseas: others might come from Bromholm, others again from the South go along the Icknield Way through Royston and Newmarket and

Fakenham. Those who passed close to Castle Acre would no doubt take time to wonder at the chief relic of the priory there, an arm of St Philip. In this place there was a small infirmary where pilgrims who had struggled thus far, and were too weak to go further, could receive the Last Sacrament. Others, pressing on, and crossing the River Wensum at Fakenham would feel with excitement that they were near their goal. When they reached Houghton St Giles, a mile or so short of the shrine, they would do what Henry VIII did, and remove their shoes at the Slipper Chapel, as it is called, before walking barefoot into Walsingham itself.

What was it they had gone to see in a place which was for hundreds of years second only to the shrine of Becket at Canterbury, and a place to which, in the Middle Ages, everyone was expected to make pilgrimage once in a lifetime? The earliest account of the origin of the Walsingham shrine is to be found in a document known as the *Pynson Ballad*. According to this, 900 years ago a widow named Rychold prayed to Our Lady to tell her in what way she could best be honoured. So she was taken in a dream to Nazareth and showed the place where Gabriel had greeted the Virgin. The Lady Rychold was told to build a house like that at Walsingham, to re-create the Santa Casa, or Home of the Virgin, and to set it up at Walsingham. The reputed site of this structure, now within the grounds of a private house known as The Abbey, was excavated and verified by some archaeological excavations as recently as 1961. It is true that there is another site of this Holy House enclosed within the Anglican shrine, but that need not for the moment confuse us. What is of immediate importance as regards the origin of the place is that the account given in the *Pynson Ballad* is not necessarily the whole story.

There was a chapel here founded five years before the Norman Conquest by one Ricoldie de Faverches which was also reputed to be an exact copy of the home of the Virgin, of which there was another in Loreto, in Italy, said to have been conveyed in a miraculous manner from Nazareth in order to escape the depredations of the infidel conquerors of the Holy Land. Therefore, throughout all these centuries there were two 'Holy Houses': one built in Walsingham at the command of the Virgin, the other borne through the air to take rest at Loreto in Italy. A

(*Over page*) Some of the estimated crowd of 10,000 who took part in a pilgrimage to the shrine of Our Lady at Walsingham, Norfolk in 1980. (*The Press Association*)

further and most important development was that it came to be believed that the Virgin herself had come to live in Norfolk as a consequence of the infidel invasion of the Holy Land. With this developed the belief that a portion of the Virgin's milk had also found its way to Walsingham. Indeed, when the scholar Erasmus visited the place, and gave an account of it in the sixteenth century, not long before the Dissolution, he records having seen it. What, therefore, those swarms of pilgrims who made their way for so many centuries to Walsingham went to see was in essence two things: the Holy House, and the Image of Our Lady which it had come to contain.

It was the Image which soon became the prime object of popular veneration, so that Our Lady of Walsingham became, and for long remained, a national figure of great sanctity. Kings and queens worshipped her, bringing gifts to her shrine. Edward IV in 1469 and his queen made pilgrimage. In 1470 John Paston – of the same family as that which lived near Bromholm – wrote to his mother to tell her that the Duchess of Norfolk would visit Norwich on her way to Walsingham. Henry VII gave a silver image of himself. Henry III, Edward I, Edward II, Henry VIII – all walked barefoot the last mile. Henry VIII is reputed to have left his soul in charge of Our Lady of Walsingham. Henry and Catherine of Aragon went there to give thanks for the birth of their child. And a letter exists written by Catherine of Aragon to Henry announcing the victory of the Battle of Flodden and concluding by telling him that she was then on her way to Walsingham to give thanks.

Walsingham in the days of its greatness is vividly described by Erasmus in his *Colloquy*, published in 1526, though it needs to be remembered that this was a skit: he had gone there as a sceptic. By the time of his visit there was a priory which had been founded in 1420 by Godfrey de Faverches and given to the Order of Augustinians, or Austen friars, to maintain, which Order also served the shrine. Pilgrims entering the priory would first pass through the narrow gate above which was a copper figure of a knight on horseback. He was said, in one of the many Walsingham legends which by this time had come into existence, to have saved his own life, when pursued by enemies, by praying to the Virgin as he approached this narrow entrance, and then finding himself able to pass through it without dismounting. After this gateway came a small chapel containing a huge bone, said to have been the finger of St Peter. The pilgrim could kiss this for a fee. Passing on he came to a building of reeds and straw which enclosed two wells said to have healing properties. Erasmus found that between the two wells there was a stone on which it was customary, for those who wished, to kneel with the right knee bared. One hand was then placed in each well until the water reached to the wrist, while the votary made his wish. After that he drank from the water as much as he could hold in the hollow of his hands. In the Chapel of the Virgin, a small wooden building with a door in each side for pilgrims coming and going stood the famous Image of the Virgin, just to the right of the altar. Erasmus saw the gold and jewels with which this figure was adorned. He also saw, at another altar, the relics of the heavenly milk, enclosed in crystal and attached to a crucifix, which he said looked remarkably like chalk mixed with white of egg. He wrote: 'As soon as the Canon in attendance saw us he rose, put on his surplice, added the stole to his neck, prostrated himself with due ceremony, and worshipped: anon he stretched forth the thrice Holy Milk to be kissed by us. On this we also, on the lowest step of the Altar, religiously fell prostrate. . .'. This, then, was Walsingham as it was, the focus of the pilgrim devotion of countless thousands of people, high and low, for many centuries.

Today the priory, now called Walsingham Abbey, may be entered by the main gate in the High Street. Above the doorway is a very odd carving of a porter's head apparently looking out of a window to see who comes. Through the gate the great arch of the East window of the Priory Church is ahead, and a very noble arch it is too. The actual site of the shrine of Our Lady – the actual site of the Holy House – lay to the north of the church. The wells, where pilgrims did their wishing, lay to the south. There is much evidence, too, of the former priory to be found in and around the walls of the present Abbey House: an undercroft, which was the warming-room underneath the dormitory and is reached by a doorway on the north side of the house: a refectory, and cloisters. In Walsingham itself there is the Common Place, an open space where stands the Pump House with a brazier on top, lit at times of particular celebration. Near by is the Shire-Hall where there is an interesting museum. On the south side of the village, alongside the Fakenham road, are the ruins of what was once the Franciscan Friary.

But to speak of ruins within the context of Walsingham is quite misleading. This place now is a living pilgrimage centre pulsating with life. 'England's Nazareth' as it has been called draws people

from the world over, a revival which is of comparatively recent date. The Anglican shrine, built between 1931 and 1937, surrounds a replica of the Holy House, visited by thousands, both individuals and in organised pilgrimages on a very large scale. The centre of Roman Catholic devotion is the Slipper Chapel at Houghton St Giles, a mile to the south of the priory. This is very impressive and evocative of all those, from royalty onwards, who through the long centuries paused there to remove their shoes and then to walk humbly onwards into Walsingham itself. Here there is a fully equipped Pilgrims' Centre where on busy days as many as 8,000 people at once can join in Mass around the covered altar. There is even a Walsingham now in the United States, founded by Americans who, returning home after the Second World War with memories of the place, opened the National Shrine of Our Lady of Walsingham in Williamsburg, Virginia.

It has to be admitted that the shrine at Walsingham is founded upon the story of a very curious event. Did the Lady Rychold really have a dream in which Our Lady asked her to build a replica of the Holy House of Nazareth in Walsingham? And, if that was so, why was another Holy House apparently carried through the air to alight upon Loreto in Italy? It is certainly the case that when the way to the Holy Land was blocked by Saracen invaders' pilgrims came instead to England's Nazareth. But – and this is an odd feature of the whole matter – it was in the fifteenth century, long after the foundation of Walsingham, that the shrine of Our Lady there reached the peak of popularity. The oddity derives from the fact that this was a terrible century, when the country was racked by troubles and tumults of all kinds, accompanied by what might be called a hardening of the arteries of the institutional Church. One writer, speaking of the popularity of Walsingham at this time has suggested that, 'It may be that it was the very decadence of the Church that caused men to seek even more than before an individual way to salvation: on the other hand, the widespread revival of magic and witchcraft following loss of faith in the Church may have sent some, as the Lollards had said, to "the Witch of Walsingham". Was it that the age of faith had finally abdicated to one of gross superstition?'

'As soon as the Canon in attendance saw us he rose . . . anon he stretched forth the thrice Holy Milk to be kissed by us.' (Erasmus and Colet at Walsingham.)

That is perhaps a rather unkind way of putting it. It cannot be just 'gross superstition' which sends people to Walsingham now. Nor, surely, could it be said of all those many who made their way there in times past. But it remains a haunting thought that the condition of the fifteenth century with its bestial Wars of the Roses, its plagues, its brutal and treacherous public life, all of which must have borne hard upon the ordinary men seeking a little peace and certainty, bears in its way not a little resemblance to our own sombre century with its ever-present nuclear threat and economic instabilities. Are not these the very circumstances which in all ages, for better or for worse, move people in pilgrimage to seek out something they can see and understand? It is at any rate an interesting thought with which to leave this endlessly fascinating place which is Walsingham.

King's Lynn and Margery Kempe

There are good reasons for finishing this journey through some of the pilgrim sites of East Anglia at Lynn. (It was not King's Lynn, incidentally, until the time of Henry VIII.) For one thing it is a fascinating place, once a great port, an important centre of the Hanseatic League of merchants who traded with the Baltic, once the home of whalers who sailed to the northern seas, as the house in the town called 'The Greenland Fishery' bears witness. Furthermore, in St Margaret's, it has a marvellous church. Even more to our purpose, it has the Red Mount Chapel a very striking and rare example of a pilgrim wayside chapel. Pilgrims would call here on the way to Walsingham to give thanks for a safe voyage across from the Continent. Sea crossings for pilgrims were always risky. There is a revealing episode in Caxton's *Dialogues in French and English*, that phrase book, mentioned earlier, for the use of pilgrims. Some of them ask the hostess of a hostel:

> 'Dame, may men go by ship from hence?'
> 'Yea, there is a ship redy full of people. God keep them in safety!'

Lynn was an important entry port for foreign pilgrims bound for Walsingham. At the Red Mount Chapel or Our Lady's Mount, as they called it, they would not only give thanks, but probably also make an act of confession. There is a priest's living-room to be seen there now, and three chapels. In Lynn itself they would have been able to find lodging at the four monastic establishments in the town, marked now by gateways of what were houses of Augustinian friars, White friars, Grey friars. There is a Blackfriars Street. And, in a town vividly evocative of mediaeval society, St Margaret's Church, with its effigies of bygone mayors and their wives, and angels playing silent music on many instruments, seems to sum it all up.

But Lynn, for those who care to think about it, also has a memory of a very remarkable pilgrim of her day – Margery Kempe. If Mother Julian in Norwich was the first woman to write a book, Margery Kempe was the first to write an autobiography – *The Book of Margery Kempe*. Born in Lynn around 1373, she lived in Saturday Market, where her birthplace may still be seen. She has been called a mystic: she has been called a religious maniac. She was subject to visions. She is one of the few pilgrims of whom we have personal knowledge. She was also noisy, extrovert and difficult to live with, as her husband discovered. Above all, and this is her significance to the pilgrim story, she was quintessentially one herself. Her travels covered virtually her lifetime, and as distinct from the Wife of Bath and her like, she was concerned with the religious motives of her many pilgrimages. She travelled widely to shrines in her native land as well as abroad. And always she believed absolutely in the genuineness of her religious experiences visiting Canterbury, Compostela, and, as her journey of a lifetime, the Holy Land itself. Her experiences on this famous journey give a good picture of what befell pilgrims making this trip. They travelled overland from the Channel coast, making frequently for Venice. There they bought space – literally space, since it was usually little more than an area on deck – on one of the ships which ran from there to Haifa or some other near-by port, such as Jaffa. Then they made their way through the coastal plain and then up and up through the hot hills to the Holy City, Jerusalem. It was dangerous, it was physically testing, it was, all things considered, an immense and courageous undertaking, and it is surprising that, through many centuries, so many made it. The rewards, on the other hand, were great, both spiritual and material: the one brought merit in Heaven, the other the reputation back home of a traveller with many tales to tell. It was also the pilgrim's ultimate crown of glory.

Margery Kempe was entranced by the Holy Land, apparently oblivious to the irritation she caused her fellow-travellers, an irritation so great that at one stage of the journey they raised a subscription among themselves to pay her to go away. By the time she had reached the Church of the Holy Sepulchre in Jerusalem she had developed, in addition to her usual sobbing and wailing, what has been called 'a prolonged and violent shriek which broke from her lips at the sight of anything holy'. Her ideas were not profound, but she has made an impression which has lasted long after her death. One writer has put it, 'she was endowed with the gift of tears and seems to have been favoured with singular signs of Christ's love'. She was certainly the most persistent pilgrim which Norfolk, that land of pilgrims, ever produced. And certainly, she possessed genuine holiness. Perhaps all that needs to be said is that it went to her head a little. But *The Book of Margery Kempe* will live, and so therefore might her memory well be recalled in Lynn, a place where the tracks of pilgrims of old are still strong.

CHAPTER 3

Through Lincolnshire to Yorkshire

Crowland – St Guthlac
Lincoln – St Hugh
Beverley – St John
York – St William
Ripon – St Wilfrid
Lastingham – St Cedd and St Chad
Whitby – Hilda and Caedmon

Crowland. Three men in a boat

On St Bartholomew's Day, 25 August 699, a sturdy man accompanied by two servants, made a cautious way by boat, skirting the reeds and poisonous marshes, on to the fenlands south of the Wash, until he came to a little island, not much more than a slight rise in the surrounding flatness, and there landed. The man's name was Guthlac: of the two servants one, acting as a guide, was called Tatwin and the other Beccelm. They had come to this desolate place because Guthlac, son of a Mercian nobleman, first a soldier, then a monk in the abbey at Repton in Derbyshire, desired to seek for himself a more secluded life. He could scarcely have made a starker choice, for even to this day Crowland is an isolated spot. Ague and all the attendant evils of a low-lying country were to assail him; the inhabitants of the island were rough and barbarous: in winter the wind cut keenly across the waste and sometimes, as now, the sea poured in from the Wash, bringing dangerous floods. What we have come to discover is why, in spite of all this, and because of Guthlac, the ruins of a once great abbey stand now in this unlikely spot.

The last time I travelled there it was a bleak March day: but the cold clarity of the wide skies made all the more startling the sudden vision of the ruins of Crowland as they came into view. It is a place strong in atmosphere: a little isolated market town with its extraordinary triangular bridge under which no water flows and from which a sermon is preached every Good Friday. To the right of this, and overshadowing all, is the abbey. The whole place speaks of the past, and the abbey, with the odd tale of its origin, seems to bring very close those far-off days when England was a country of petty kingdoms, with Mercia one of the largest, having a court and a royal mausoleum at that Repton from which Guthlac came.

The facts behind the foundation of so great an abbey in so unlikely a spot are striking. Late in the seventh century a prince of Mercia named Ethelbald found his way to Crowland as a fugitive from the fury of a cousin who was resisting his attempts to obtain the throne. On the island he found the cell in which by this time Guthlac was living as a hermit. He also found, in the man himself, who by this time had been spiritually matured by the solitary life he had sought, someone who could give him wise counsel and advice. Guthlac, indeed, did more: he prophesied that Ethelbald the fugitive would in due time succeed to the throne of Mercia. In return, Ethelbald vowed that, if the hermit's words came true, then he would erect a monastery on the spot where he had benefited so much from the friendship of Guthlac. The Saint died on the Wednesday in Passion Week, 11 April 714. Two years later, on St Bartholomew's Day, Ethelbald fulfilled his vow and laid the foundation stone of the abbey, at the same time endowing it with land and money and dedicating it to the glory of God, Our Lady and St Bartholomew. Thus, this abbey came to exist in the isolation of the Lincolnshire Fens.

Of outstanding interest is the quatrefoil over the west door of the nave, showing incidents in the life of Guthlac: in one leaf he is landing on the island, with Tatwin and Beccelm. And because it had been revealed in a dream that where they landed they would find a sow under a willow tree with a litter of white pigs, these can be made out in the now crumbling carving. The left leaf shows the ordination of Guthlac by Headda, Bishop of Winchester; in the centre the Saint is compelling Satan to bring stone for the abbey; on the right is depicted the laying out of Guthlac's body in a shroud; and in the uppermost can be seen the apotheosis of the Saint. Above the west door of the abbey is a rich array of statues: four of them of particular interest, King Ethelbald, the founder,

An illustration from the Guthlac Roll in the British Museum, showing Guthlac, saint and hermit being ferried across to the island of Crowland in the Lincolnshire Fens. Tatwin, his guide, is at the tiller, and his servant Beccelm in the prow of the Saxon boat. (*The British Library*)

St Bartholomew, patron saint of the abbey with the knife which is the symbol of his martyrdom and St Guthlac himself holding a whip of discipline, which in itself is a grim reminder of one of the hazards of the solitary life – the temptations of the flesh. Today, we should no doubt call these sexual fantasies; but they were real enough and hard enough to bear.

The floor of Guthlac's cell was excavated in 1908, but has since been covered in, though its position is indicated by the metal label on the west of the South aisle. Also in the abbey is to be found a skull bearing clear marks of a wound inflicted from behind as if by a blade which emerged through the eye socket. There is a belief that this is the skull of one of the early abbots of Crowland who was murdered by the Danes in the course of one of their raids some time between 716 and 860, which led to the destruction of the first abbey.

A second was built between 948 and 975, a third in the twelfth century, portions of which can still be seen, especially in the fine Norman dogtooth West arch of the central tower. Earthquake and fire led to the destruction of this, and a fourth was created between 1392 and 1469, which continued until the Dissolution of 1539, all of which shows how persistent was the memory and how strong the attraction of Guthlac the Hermit. A series of eighteen curious pictures of incidents from his life are contained in the Guthlac Roll, kept now in the British Museum.

Crowland is an odd place which still draws its pilgrims; of whom I was glad to be one. There was not a soul to be seen that bleak morning when I was last there. But there did seem a presence to be felt in the atmosphere of the place – that of Guthlac, of long ago.

Lincoln and St Hugh

The A15 across the wide Lincolnshire wolds, which was the route I followed on a recent visit, dips into Lincoln itself, thus emphasising the grandeur of the situation of the vast cathedral which stands on a hill overlooking the town. To reach the cathedral it is necessary to walk the last stages of approach up steep narrow and winding cobbled streets, a way taken by many pilgrims of the past and many, if not more, now.

Lincoln itself was a Roman city of great importance. Ermine Street, the great Roman way to the North, leads straight as a ruler from it. And when long afterwards a Norman monk named Remigius came here in order to begin the building of the Cathedral Church of the Blessed Virgin Mary of Lincoln in 1072,

The West Front of Lincoln Cathedral. This has been called one of the most impressive façades in the world. Many pilgrims climbed the hill inspired by devotion to St Hugh, whose head shrine can still be seen. There is a carving of a Lincoln pilgrim over the eastern window of the chapel under the south-west tower. (*A. F. Kersting*)

he found a Danish and Saxon population living on top of the hill within the ruined walls of the Roman city. He also found there a minster church, that is to say a central church with a body of clergy under discipline who travelled out for services in distant country places where no parochial system had been established. This is why the term Lincoln Minster has survived and why there is still a Minster Yard adjoining it. However, Remigius, who had given considerable financial support to William the Conqueror, and who was the first Norman to be rewarded with an English bishopric, removed this minster, together with the Danes and Saxons living around, leaving the site clear for the building of the Norman cathedral. It was consecrated shortly after the death of Remigius, in 1092.

But it did not last long. In 1141 the wooden roof was destroyed by fire and reconstructed in stone at the orders of the third Bishop of Lincoln, Alexander the Magnificent. It was he who was responsible for the embellishment of the western doors and the insertion in the façade of the carved frieze which is now one of the most striking possessions of the cathedral. It deserves a long and thoughtful look, suggesting, as it does, the gateway to Heaven itself. But this façade, the West wall, and the western towers were all that survived from a fire in 1141 and, strangely enough, from an earthquake which in the following year shook the hill of Lincoln, bringing down all the rest of the building. So Lincoln had yet again to be rebuilt, and it is this which brings upon the scene a man central to the whole history and life of this place right up to this present time – St Hugh of Lincoln.

Hugh was one of the three children of a lord of Avalon, and was born in a castle at Pontcharra near Grenoble, on the borders of Savoy. His biographer, Brother Adam, a monk like himself, dwells with pride upon this aristocratic lineage. But this did not prevent Hugh, accustomed as he was to the ways of courts, to wish ardently for the religious life in its most extreme form of renunciation. It was this desire which made him seek entry into the toughest religious order of the day, the Carthusians, whose mother-house was set in a grim situation at La Grande Chartreuse in the Alps. It is said that when Hugh spoke to an old monk here about his intention, the man looked grimly at his pale face and delicate limbs and told him he was a fool, saying, 'the men who inhabit these rocks are as hard as the rocks themselves. They have no mercy on their own bodies and none on others. The dress will scrape the flesh from your bones. The discipline will tear the bones themselves out of such frail limbs as yours.'

Yet Hugh persisted, and into this Order, whose monks were vowed to silence, who each lived in his own cell, who each devoted several hours daily to mental prayer and whose physical circumstances, as regards food and clothing were of the sparsest possible kind, he was eventually admitted. This was the man who was brought to England by Henry II to be Prior of the then recently founded Carthusian house at Witham in Somerset. Subsequently, and by the same King, and much against his will, he was summoned to the bishopric of Lincoln. Thus, it fell to him, and to his clerk of the works, Geoffrey de Noyers, to begin the work of rebuilding the cathedral, which he did with vigour and creative imagination, presenting for posterity the great masterpiece which stands to this day basically unaltered except for certain additions made in the time of another notable bishop, Robert Grosseteste.

Hugh was much given throughout his life to austerities: he was brave – his monkish biographer describes him as 'fearless as a lion' – which indeed he needed to be to face up to such alarming Plantagenet kings as Henry II and Richard Coeur de Lion. He was also a wise statesman, in that age when bishops, especially one who ruled over so vast an area as the Diocese of Lincoln then was, needed also to be high officers of state. His courage was also shown in that he twice faced violent anti-Jewish mobs intent on pillage and murder. And, though he was a man of peppery temper himself, there does seem to have been a gentler side to his nature, as the queer story of the swan, which is one of his emblems, testifies. It is best told by the historian J. A. Froude:

Like all genuine men, the Bishop was an object of special attraction to children and animals. The little ones in every house that he entered were always found clinging about his legs. Of the attachment of other creatures to him, there was one very singular instance. About the time of his Installation there appeared on the mere at Stow Manor, eight miles from Lincoln, a swan of unusual size, which drove the other male birds off the water . . . this bird, on the occasion of the Bishop's first visit to the Mano, was brought to him to be seen as a curiosity. He was usually unmanageable and savage; but the Bishop knew the way to his heart; fed him, and taught him him to poke his head into the pockets of his frock to look for breadcrumbs. Ever after he seemed to know instinctively

when the Bishop was expected, flew trumpetting up and
down the lake, slapping the water with his wings; when the
horses approached, he would march out upon the grass to
meet them; strutted at the Bishop's side, and would
sometimes follow him upstairs.

And yet there was another side to Hugh, one which illustrates
vividly how much he was a man of his times. On a visit to the
Abbey of Fécamp in Normandy he was shown a precious relic of
that place, the reputed arm of St Mary Magdalen. Undoing the
bandages in which it was wrapped, Hugh first tried to break off a
finger from the hand and then, failing to do this, chewed away
two pieces of a finger which he calmly handed to his monkish
attendant. When remonstrated with he said, 'If a little while ago I
handled the sacred body of the Lord with my fingers in spite of
my unworthiness, and partook of it with my lips and teeth, why
should I not treat the bones of the saints in the same way?'

Hugh died in 1200 and was canonised in 1220. Already as the
reputation of his holy life spread, a pilgrim cult had begun. His
remains, which were held to have great healing powers, were
translated to the chapel behind the high altar in 1280. None of this
now remains; but there is a singular structure in the beautiful
angel choir – so called because of the figures of angels carved in
the spandrels above. This is the head shrine of Hugh, the place
where the Saint's head was kept as a subsidiary shrine to the
main one. The pavement in front of it is much worn, as though
many pilgrims passed that way and no doubt knelt. It is on record
that in the fourteenth century the jewelled reliquary which
contained the head was stolen; but the skull was left in a near-by
window, where a black crow stood guard until the monks arrived
to replace it.

In the great days of the cult wealthy Lincoln citizens assisted
destitute pilgrims who had made their way to the shrine. When a
cure occurred, these benefactors would be fetched to witness that
which had been thus assisted by their charity. And here, as
elsewhere, the saying of paternosters often accompanied the
healing process. A pilgrim would recite nine such paternosters as
he knelt with his afflicted arm or leg or other member when
possible thrust through one of the apertures of the shrine. At

'When the horses approached he would march out upon the grass to meet them.'
(The swan of St Hugh of Lincoln.)

Lincoln some effort was made to test cures to see if they were genuine. One case was that of a woman who arrived with clenched fists which were locked in that position, whereupon the Sub-Dean tried to prise them open to see if this was a genuine affliction, which apparently it was, fairly obviously belonging to those psychosomatic conditions which were particularly open, as indeed they still are, to healing suggestion. Sometimes, here as elsewhere, pilgrims in search of a cure would spend a long time, days, weeks, even months, at the tomb waiting for miracles to happen. One case at Lincoln was that of a woman from the town of Beverley in Yorkshire who was apparently cured of her affliction. Even so, the Sub-Dean sent messengers the 45 miles to Beverley to enquire of the chapter of Beverley Minster as to whether to their knowledge this woman had been genuinely afflicted. The answer they received there, as in the adjoining villages where they also enquired, was affirmative, whereupon the cure at Lincoln was pronounced genuine.

There are other places for pilgrims to visit at Lincoln, including the tomb of Bishop Grosseteste, who, although uncanonised, was also revered as a saint. And in the South choir aisle, where it can still be seen, was the sad shrine of Little St Hugh – yet another example of that manic anti-Semitism which was a curse of the Middle Ages. The story closely follows that of St William of Norwich, except that here, in the case of Little St Hugh, the child's body, discovered in a cess-pit near some Jewish house, was held to represent a Jewish murder for ritual purposes. The body, apparently, cried out from its burial-place, and so led people to it. The Prioress in Chaucer's *Canterbury Tales* piously repeats this slanderous nonsense which apparently because she says 'it is but a litel while ago' had just begun to get around. It is good to remember that great St Hugh faced up on several occasions to anti-Jewish rioters.

Such are some of the thoughts and some of the memories with which today's pilgrim may well go around this wonderful place. But there are two figures, one easily found, one which has to be sought after, which should on no account be missed. The first is the striking statue of Edward King, a nineteenth-century bishop whose radiant personality and love for people was outstanding in his day and has been remembered since. The statue, which stands in the south transept under the magnificent round window called 'The Bishop's Eye' was paid for by many subscriptions large and small which came from admirers all over

England. It is pleasant to think that he, and the great St Hugh, would have found in each other much to respect. To find the second figure it is necessary to go outside the cathedral and to look up at the tracery over the eastern window of the chapel which projects under the South-western tower. There is a lovely little carving of a Lincoln pilgrim, complete with staff and burden on his back, the very image and prototype of countless folk who made their way up the hill to reach the cathedral and, indeed, of their modern counterparts who still do.

The kindly Saint of Beverley

I shall not easily forget those primroses, massed around the grave slab in the huge fourteenth-century nave beneath which lie the remains of Beverley's saint called by Bede 'A Holy man named John'. Every year the flowers are placed there on his birthday by the children of the village school at Harpham on the Wolds, where he was born thirteen centuries ago. Thus, across an enormous range of time has his memory persisted, and though all traces of his shrine have gone, and though pilgrims no longer come, as once they did, to seek healing at it, yet the children of his native place nurture this kindly memory of him. So, in an entirely different way, does the vast minster which exists because of him. So it is this astonishingly continuous remembrance, as well as the splendours of the place, which make a visit here now so rewarding.

Yet anyone who comes here now, as many do, must wonder how so great a church has risen in so comparatively small a place. The answer is to be found in the reputation for holiness which John of Beverley acquired and with the miracles associated with his name both in his lifetime and afterwards. It is a strange story, all the stranger by reason of the sometimes fanciful additions which later chroniclers, such as William of Malmesbury brought to it. But Bede knew him in the flesh: indeed, the Monk of Jarrow had been ordained deacon and priest by John, and writes of him with real affection. By the time Bede met him, John, who had been trained and brought up in the famous 'double monastery' at Whitby under Abbess Hilda, was Bishop of Hexham. It is with the account of a touching happening during John's time at Hexham that Bede begins his account of him. For Bede, the tale

Beverley Minster, an enormous building in a small town, sprang from the holiness and fame of St John of Beverley, who is buried in the nave. Bede records miracles performed by John, whose relics drew many pilgrims to his shrine. (*A. F. Kersting*)

obviously records a miracle. For us, it may well stand as the first instance we have of John's endearing compassion.

During Lent, and at other times when he had opportunity, Bede records, it was John's custom to go aside into the country near his church at Hexham, there to pray and live quietly with a few companions. At the same time he always made it a rule that some poor person of the neighbourhood should be sought out and brought into their circle, in order to receive their charity. One Lent, the person brought in was a youth from a distant village who, in addition to being unable to speak, was also afflicted with scabs and scales all over his bald head. Bede goes on:

> When one week of Lent was past, on the following Sunday John told the poor lad to come to him, and when he had entered he ordered him to put out his tongue and show it him. Then he took him by the chin, and making the sign of the Holy Cross on his tongue, told him to retract it and speak. 'Pronounce some word', he said: 'say yea', which is the English word of agreement and assent. The lad's tongue was loosed, and at once he did what he was told. The Bishop then proceeded to the names of letters: 'Say A.' And he said 'A'. 'Now say B', he said, which the youth did, and when he had repeated the names of each of the letters after the Bishop, the latter added syllables and words for him to repeat after him.

By persevering in this way John taught the lad first more words, then a few phrases, then whole sentences so that 'as long as he could keep awake, the youth never stopped saying something and expressing his own inner thoughts and wishes, which he had never been able to do previously'. Delighted with this cure, John ordered his physician to treat the lad's scabby head, which before long was cleared up, so that he 'obtained a clear complexion, readiness of speech, and a beautiful head of hair'.

There is a ring of truth here. The picture is almost a perfect one of a familiar figure of the rough society of those times, an outcast spurned because of physical disabilities, yet needing only a little kindness to make him whole. There were always many such to be found among the pilgrim throngs of those and later centuries seeking healing at some shrine or well. This lad found it at the hands of a holy man.

Bede records other miracles of John, all performed during his lifetime. There was the occasion when, after he had left Hexham to become Bishop of York, as the see was at that time called, he visited a convent where one of the nuns, having recently been bled in the arm, was suffering acutely from what seems to have been an acute case of septicaemia. However, John, having first reprimanded the Abbess for allowing the blood-letting to take place 'on the fourth day of the moon', prayed over the girl, who soon was healed. On another occasion, being strongly pressed to do so, he sent to a sick woman some of the Holy Water which he had blessed for the dedication of a church, giving instructions that she was to drink of it and also to apply some to the place where the worst pain was. Again, the patient was cured.

So this much-loved man, trained long ago at Abbess Hilda's monastery at Whitby, subsequently Bishop of Hexham and then of York, came to Beverley, then called In-Derawuda to end his days 'in a manner pleasing to God' as Bede puts it. He died in 721, having resigned his bishopric and settled in what was then a small monastery in a remote and thinly populated countryside. But legend and miracle continued to be associated with his name. Like many other saints, especially those of these early days, he was reputed to have particular *rapport* with animals. Thus it was recorded, by William of Malmesbury, that the cruel sport of bull-baiting could not be carried on in the churchyard at Beverley, because the memory of the Saint's relics lying nearby was such that the dogs became too gentle to attack. At the same time, and by contrast, his intercession was held to be particularly powerful in military matters. When King Athelstan in the early tenth century passed on his way to wage war against the Scots, he paused at Beverley, leaving his dagger on the altar as a pledge of his promise to endow the church if he were victorious. Much later, in 1137, St John's banner was carried at the Battle of the Standard, when again the Scots were the enemy, and again by the army of Edward I when he drove the same adversary back across the border. Most strikingly of all, it was believed that, on the morning of the Battle of Agincourt, holy oil seeped from the shrine of St John in token of the victory which was to follow, a victory so great that Henry V in gratitude made costly gifts to the shrine.

This is the background which can make a total experience of a visit to Beverley Minster today. Much was to happen in that place from the time of the death of John to the completion of the great building which is there now. Inevitably, the place suffered terribly in the years of Viking conquest. Lying close to the Humber, up which their long ships could conveniently come, it was one of the first to suffer. Later, in times of comparative peace, King Athelstan, who had left his dagger on the altar, refounded the church and the monastery, which became very important in the years before the Norman Conquest. By that time a rich gold and silver shrine contained the relics of John. Thereafter followed through the centuries the customary alternations of disasters and recoveries which are so often part of the story of any great mediaeval building. A great fire in 1188 destroyed much of the town and church. It was not in fact known what happened on this occasion until the chance discovery of a sheet of lead in a vault in 1664, which recorded the fact that nine years after this fire a search was made for John's relics, which were duly restored. In 1213, the great central tower which the canons had unwisely decided to increase in size, collapsed, the brethren escaping only because, on that particular day, the bell for service was rung one hour earlier than usual.

The tremendous building which stands there now was complete by 1420, including the two great western towers which are such a feature of Beverley. The whole place is a memorial to John: all through the centuries it was the continuing stream of pilgrims to his shrine which made the building possible. This shrine stood on top a screen behind the high altar and there, quite clearly, its site can be made out today, together with the little stairway up which pilgrims climbed from the North choir aisle to get to it. There is a carved face on the right of the doorway giving on to this North choir aisle which is said to have been the place where a lamp was kept, very likely for use by pilgrims climbing the dark stairs to the shrine. Beverley Minster is rich in detail such as this, and today's pilgrim has his choice of many. There is the Fridstol, a stone seat upon which, when some terrified fugitive, seeking shelter within the minster precincts, came to state his case, an official would sit to hear him. Or there is the extraordinary series of carvings of mediaeval musicians, each with a separate instrument, in the North aisle of the nave, or the series of figures depicting common mediaeval ailments, from toothache to sciatica, near by.

But for me the most marvellous creation in this place is the tomb standing to the north of the sanctuary, said to be that of the Lady Eleanor, wife of Henry, first Lord Percy. This canopy, too, has been described as one of the glories of mediaeval European art, with its beautifully carved canopy overflowing with rich detail. But the most memorable thing for me is the tender carving of a small figure, representing the soul of a woman, placed upon the knee of a Christ figure who is receiving her above the tomb. Angels are removing her winding sheet and the Lord is placing his hand, as though in welcome or blessing, upon her head. I like to feel, somehow, that this would have particularly appealed to John of Beverley, upon whose grave, every May, the children of his native village place those primroses.

A true pilgrimage to York

It was obvious at a glance that the lid on the stone coffin of St William did not fit, but lay somewhat at an angle. It is an unwieldy object, unquestionably Roman, apart from the ill-fitting lid. Just as the monks at Ely found a Roman sarcophagus at Grantchester in which to place the body of St Etheldreda, so, when William was buried in 1154, this one, 7 feet long and weighing about a ton, was brought from the Roman cemetery in York. When the existing nave of the minster was built in later centuries, the floor level rose and the coffin was hidden from view. It was found again when, in the middle of the eighteenth century, a local historian uncovered it. Inside was a lead box containing bones. The coffin was not disturbed again until the huge restoration works of 1967–72 when, because of engineering work on the foundations of the central tower, it had to be moved. It rests now in the Western crypt. So, historically speaking, it is in the wrong place, it does not with any certainty contain the true relics of the saint, its lid does not fit, and it is not possible to visit it without first obtaining the services of a guide, who will unlock the crypt and take you down.

There seemed something deeply symbolic about all this: indicative of the fact that no true pilgrimage to this wonderful place which is York Minster should begin with St William, or even have him primarily in mind. He is rather a dim saint: no strong memory of him as a person, such as that which carried the name of, for instance, John of Beverley through the centuries, is associated with this man's name. Even his claims to sanctity seem to rest upon slight foundations, and there are strong indications that his canonisation in 1227 was probably pressed by the minster authorities as some kind of riposte to the huge popularity of the cult of St Thomas at Canterbury where, in 1220, there had been a great ceremony at which the body of St Thomas was transferred from the crypt of Canterbury Cathedral into its great new shrine.

Yet William did attract pilgrims in considerable numbers

through the years. His tomb originally stood at the eastern end of the nave, where it could readily be seen by those entering. Subsequently, in 1284, it was moved to a great shrine behind the high altar, which shrine probably consisted of a silver coffin elevated on a tall marble pedestal. Some of the interesting sculpture which once adorned this tomb can be seen now in the Yorkshire Museum in York.

There is nothing very inspiring even about the story of William. Born to the purple, as son of the chancellor and treasurer of Henry I, he held a post of treasurer of the cathedral of York and in 1141 was elected archbishop. Those were the days of ecclesiastical power politics: William's election was disputed; he was removed from office, thereupon retiring to Winchester where his uncle the Bishop received him into the monastery. His claims to sanctity would appear to rest upon the marked humility with which he accepted this reverse, remaining 'with the monks in regularity and retirement, uncomplaining and without a word of reproach against his opponents'. He was reinstated, after pleading his cause at Rome, some years later and returned to York in the May of 1154. The first of various miracles attributed to him occurred on this occasion. When he was being escorted into the city by a great crowd the Ouse Bridge which his company was crossing collapsed, drowning many people. One of the carvings in the Yorkshire Museum, once a part of his shrine, actually shows this scene. But William's prayers restored the casualties to life. But it was a short-lived triumph. William died some three weeks later after being taken violently ill while celebrating Mass, and the dark rumour lived on for a long time that he had been poisoned.

Such is the tale of St William. Quite obviously, it is a totally inadequate beginning for any search for the glories and the splendours which are York. That is why, for my part, I left that crypt to search elsewhere. I went down into the undercroft.

This is a place of extraordinary interest, the existence of which was virtually unknown until recent years. Then, because the great towers of York were seen to be sinking, and much of the great building in serious danger of collapse, it was found necessary to excavate this space in order, by means of brilliant engineering techniques, to prop up the foundations so that the place would stand for posterity. In so doing the discovery was made that the minster stands across and above what was once the Roman garrison of a place which they had made their military headquarters in Britain. They called it Eboracum. The archaeologists, who worked alongside the engineers during the excavation of this area, found many traces of this Roman occupation, including marvellous coloured mosaic upon one wall. The pilgrim now, looking at this, can, if he wishes, begin to hear from the far past, the trumpets of the legions, the tramp of marching feet, the rumble of chariots, and the murmur of the Roman city all about. Eboracum was of immense importance for the Romans: on two occasions, when emperors had taken up residence here, the whole far-flung Empire was administered from this place. And from time to time, among all these echoes of the past, sounds can be picked up of significance in the Christian story. The Emperor Severus who descended upon Verulamium – the St Albans of later times – to persecute Christians and left one of his sons, Geta, in that place to carry out his orders, was on his way to Eboracum, where he set up his court for a time. Above all, it was here, that Constantine the Great, the first Christian Emperor, was acclaimed in 306.

There was a Christian community, however rudimentary, in York thenceforth. The first mention of a bishop of York occurs in the Acts of the Council of Arles when a small and poor delegation arrived from the Church in Britain to that continental gathering. But this original Christian community was inevitably wiped out in the Saxon invasions. The faith returned to York when, in 625, Paulinus, consecrated Bishop of York, baptised the Northumbrian King, Edwin, on Easter Eve, in the year 627. A small wooden oratory was built for this occasion. Where it stood is not exactly known; but it was certainly within the precincts of the present great minster, the first of many notable Christian occasions to take place there.

This baptism of King Edwin is an interesting story in itself. The Romans had withdrawn their troops about the year 380. From that time until the end of the sixth century little is known of what was happening in Britain. Then, in 597, an event of the utmost significance, before long to have its effects in York also, took place on the coast of Kent. There, at Ebbafleet, a party of some forty Benedictine monks, led by one, Augustine, landed as emissaries from Pope Gregory I, who had sent them. Among Augustine's party was a monk called Paulinus, who, when Edwin of Northumbria desired to marry the Princess Ethelburga, daughter of Ethelbert of Kent, was sent with her to the heathen lands of the North in order to act as her chaplain and to evangelise among the

Northumbrians. For this purpose he was consecrated Bishop and set off in the Princess's entourage.

But the Northumbrians proved difficult people to persuade. The whole country north of the Humber was then wholly pagan. How Edwin was eventually persuaded to turn to Christianity is a beautiful and well-known story, which has been often repeated but never better told than by Bede, who set it down in the first place. Edwin had gathered his thanes together to consider the claims of the new faith. The Council was held at Goodmanham, near York. The King laid the choice before them. Bede's description of how one member of this Council spoke is memorable:

> Your Majesty, when we compare the present life of man on earth with that time of which we have no knowledge, it seems to me like the swift flight of a single sparrow through the banqueting hall where you are sitting at dinner on a winter's day with your Thanes and Counsellors. In the midst there is a comforting fire to warm the hall; outside, the storms of winter rain or snow are raging. This sparrow flies swiftly in through one door of the hall, and out through another. While he is inside, he is safe from the winter storm; but after a few moments of comfort, he vanishes from sight into the wintry world from which he came. Even so, man appears on earth for a little while; but of what went before this life or of what follows, we know nothing. Therefore, if this new teaching has brought any more certain knowledge, it seems only right that we should follow it.

That indeed is what happened. Edwin's baptism in the wooden oratory took place and, shortly afterwards, to the satisfaction of Pope Gregory, who had planned that York should be the northern ecclesiastical capital, a minster was dedicated in the name of St Peter. From then on, through many changes and chances, and many hard times, the Christianity which had come from Augustine's mission, had its centre in York.

It is true that Edwin's kingdom of Northumbria soon came to disaster. Penda, King of Mercia, the scourge of Christianity in England, allied himself with a Welsh prince and defeated Edwin at the Battle of Heathfield, near Doncaster. Paulinus, believing that his guardianship of the Queen was more important than anything else, fled south with her. Everything which he had

begun in York, including the noble church of stone which he had begun again, upon the site of the present minster, was left in the hands of a deacon called James who, with extreme bravery, held on for thirty years until, indeed, Oswald, Edwin's nephew, at the Battle of Heavenfield, near Hexham, restored the situation and once more united the two northern kingdoms in one. Such in outline is some of the background to the beginnings of the present great minster at York. Whoever goes on pilgrimage to marvel at its splendours now, and who wishes to make a true pilgrimage of his visit, does well to have some of this tale in mind.

The present building was quite unknown to these distant figures of Saxon England who began the long story with the little oratory where Edwin was baptised or the comparatively small minster which followed it, or the stone church which follows that. This last, indeed, was removed by St Wilfrid, whom we shall encounter at Ripon, in 670. But it was destroyed during the Norman Conquest, a singularly disastrous time for this part of England. The Ravaging of the North, a brutal scorched-earth policy carried out by the conquerors in reply to an attempted insurrection of the conquered, was terribly severe, laying waste great areas of this part of the country. Yet, such is the tremendous Christian story of York, that during the centuries before the Conquest the place was already of much importance to Christian civilisation, at a time when much of that civilisation, in England and on the Continent, was being threatened by Viking invasions. At York, indeed, in the eighth century was the great Alcuin, tutor and adviser to the Emperor Charlemagne. Incidentally, it was he who remarked that it was 'better to copy the example of the saints than to carry about their bones', a statement which shows how strong was the cult of relics, and how much open to criticism, even in that early time. York Minster in Alcuin's day had a library famous throughout Europe. Yet nothing remains of the church of that day although, recently, the plan of a Norman minster begun in 1070 by the first Norman Archbishop, Thomas of Bayeux, has been revealed by excavation. It was built across part of the ruins of the Roman headquarters building, itself revealed in the undercroft.

York Minster, in all its glory as the pilgrim can see it now, was not even begun until the 1220s. Moreover, the building of it took

'Edwin had brought his thanes together to consider the new faith.' (Edwin at York.)

250 years, so that such people as Walter de Gray, archbishop from 1216 to 1255, could have had no hope ever of seeing the completion of the enterprise. How, and by what infinitely prolonged stages the minster was completed the pilgrim to it can readily enough discover as he explores the place now. There is so much to see, so much to marvel at, from the huge nave, the glorious choir with its remarkable screen, the fourteenth-century chapter-house, and, not to be missed, the wonderful outside view of the minster, that to make the most of a pilgrimage here it is necessary to make some personal selection of what the chief glories are. For me, beyond any doubt, it is the glass.

There is in York, if we include not only what is in the minster but also the glass in some of the parish churches as well, what has been called the greatest concentration of mediaeval stained and painted glass in England. There was in fact in the city in the later Middle Ages a school of glass painters of great fame. Some of the windows in the minster were created by this school. Others, such as the enormous and unforgettable East window came from other hands. But the sum total of them adds up to an experience of beauty and of inspiration in this form scarcely to be equalled anywhere else. To look upon it now is a reminder of how much came, in the fullness of time, from the insight of that thane who moved King Edwin of Northumbria towards baptism by speaking of his vision of the sparrow which flew out of the darkness into the light of a fire and then vanished into darkness again.

Wilfrid at Ripon

On the Saturday of the first week in August every year a citizen of Ripon dressed as a Saxon bishop rides through the town on a white horse. A curfew is still rung every evening at 9 p.m. in this history-conscious little town and a horn is blown at the same time. They have been doing this for 1,000 years; but the Bishop on the white horse is commemorating a man renowned in Ripon to this day, yet whose life was lived more than 1,000 years ago. His name was Wilfrid. Many pilgrims went to his shrine, which filled up the space behind the high altar, according to custom, in the Middle Ages. A notable figure in his day, he became the centre of a cult after it. In him is to be encountered both Celtic Christianity, which came down from the North, and that Roman Christianity which Augustine brought to Kent and which sent Paulinus to York.

Wilfrid was trained in Celtic Christianity at Lindisfarne, but became in due course a fervent admirer of the Roman way of doing things. So in him the two streams meet, and because these two streams are very important for this story, and because henceforth as we move on we shall be meeting with traces of many of the characters in this drama, it is important to pause in Ripon and find what is the importance for pilgrim's England of these two streams.

First it is important to see what England was like in Wilfrid's day. To see what had been happening to this land we now call England during the obscure centuries between the withdrawal of the Romans and the coming of the first Christian missionaries both Celtic, from the North, and Roman from the South.

What had happened in that dark time was the Saxon Conquest. It was a brutal invasion, attended with much human tragedy, and spread over many years of battle, murder and sudden death for many an isolated community left behind to live their lives in what they hoped would be peace, when the Romans withdrew. The Saxons, who were basically farmers, came across the sea first in small boat-loads looking for loot, and later in much larger parties looking for land to settle. There is some analogy between this and the conquest of the American West. In both cases land-hungry pioneers moved into the territory of a native people, and either subjugated them or drove them out, or both. The native British were the Indians of the Saxon Conquest. Many were murdered; more driven westward, some over the sea.

The land the Saxons came to was heavily wooded, wild, marshy and thinly populated. That is a point which needs constantly to be borne in mind when trying to get a picture of England in these early times. Here and there were to be found traces of the Romans: their wonderful roads, their imposing, but ruined, colonnaded streets, and forums of their deserted towns. The Saxon invaders feared these and would never settle among them, but kept their distance, thinking of them as ghost haunted.

So the invaders set themselves up in villages, each with its headman and its surrounding land, which they had hacked out of the forest and cultivated on the strip principle. Not utterly barbaric by any means, they had their own culture and civilisation. The Court where Etheldreda, later the Saint of Ely, presided with her husband, and wore her handsome necklaces, would be a fair sample of their developed life. Gods, such as Woden and Thor, Tiw and Freya – from whom we take the name of four of our weekdays – were as fierce as those who worshipped them. These, then, who by the end of the sixth century had united England into what was known as the Seven Kingdoms of the Heptarchy, were the people to whom the earliest Christian missionaries, both from the North and South, directed their efforts. And Ripon, or Rhypum, was one of their settlements. It is not possible to make full sense of the story of Ripon without first discovering more about this Celtic Christianity which came down from the North.

During the years of the Saxon Conquest, when Britain was being settled by these fierce invaders, Ireland was spared. It therefore followed that the light of Christian civilisation was kept alive in the monasteries of Ireland. So it was from these Christian centres that the movement began to evangelise heathen Northumbria and to take back across the seas the faith which their fathers had received from Patrick and which they had themselves developed and enriched. This movement came by way of Iona, the little, and to this day spirit-haunted, island off western Scotland, where Columba, coming from Ireland, founded a monastery in 563. From there this movement, represented by little bands of monks, moved across to the east coast to the island of Lindisfarne. Aidan, sent to evangelise the savage Northumbrians after Colman, an earlier emissary of Columba, had failed, set up his headquarters there. So Lindisfarne became not only a spiritual powerhouse, it also contained a school for boys, which included Wilfrid, the Saxon Bishop whom the citizens of Ripon represent every year on that white horse. He became Abbot in succession to Eata, who had been sent from Melrose.

Eata, who was very much a Celtic Christian, had brought with him the characteristics of that tradition: its simplicity, its devotion to poverty and its preference for simple ceremonies and buildings.

The reason for his departure from Ripon, and his succession by Wilfrid was a very important happening. As the years had passed, the influence of Roman Christianity which had come to these shores with Augustine, had been growing. The choice which now increasingly presented itself to the monarchs and their people of the Saxon kingdoms was, therefore, Rome or

Iona. There was far more to the difference between the two, and far more involved in the choice between the two, than the issues which were customarily presented as standing between them: the date of Easter and the form of the tonsure affected by the clergy. What was really involved was a change from the simple and primitive form of Christianity characteristic of the Celtic strain, and the discipline, the power and the enormous reputation for splendour which came from Rome. So Wilfrid was appointed to succeed Eata because he was already well known as an ardent supporter of all things Roman, and had already been to Rome not many years before. It was the first of three journeys he was to make to the Eternal City in the course of his stormy life. That is one reason why he was the representative of the Romanising party at the Great Council of Whitby which took place in 664. Three years before, when he moved in state from York into Ripon, he brought with him the manners and outlook of a man who had already been enormously impressed by what he had found in Rome. There he had found ceremonial, splendours of all kinds, the music of the Gregorian chant sounding through great stone buildings the like of which he had never seen or heard before. Thus was this Saxon moved to inaugurate important church building in the wilds of the North. While he was Bishop of York he built two churches, at Ripon and Hexham, which were regarded at the time as the finest buildings west of the Alps. It is not possible to know at this distance of time precisely what they were like, because most of Wilfrid's creations at Ripon and Hexham were destroyed by the Danish, or Viking invasions 200 years later. But in Ripon, as at Hexham, very curious crypts have survived. In Ripon, the stone crypt is the first place which should be visited. The steps down to it are on the south side of the nave. They lead to small chambers, and a narrow way leads to another staircase out of the crypt. There is a small hole on the north side which came in time to be known as Wilfrid's Needle and it was at one time supposed to be a proof of chastity to be able to creep through this hole and emerge into the passage outside, a legend which suggests the practice, common in early mediaeval times, of trial by ordeal.

But it is far more than such a tale which makes this crypt at Ripon so memorable. Its original purpose was to serve as a storehouse for the many relics which Wilfrid brought back from his three journeys to Rome. There were, of course, relics to be had in the Saxon church; but those coming from Rome had, it appears, a superior *cachet*. It was recorded by Eddie Stephen, Wilfrid's biographer, that with aid of the relics which he purchased on his first journey there, he was enabled to journey safely home, no small point, given perils and hardships of such a journey. On his second and third visits he came by still more, obtaining them, it is recorded, from 'elect' men; reliable dealers. The purpose for which he required them was for the consecration of the many churches which he desired to create in the North. These relics, which were most probably pieces of bone or objects in some way associated with saints whose reputation was high in Rome, were stored in this crypt. When the nature of the contents of the crypt became known it became a shrine.

So at Ripon Wilfrid built a great and famous church just as, for that matter, he restored the Cathedral Church of St Peter at York which he found virtually in ruins when he came to it. The subsequent history of Ripon was as tempestuous as that of Wilfrid's own life. He became Bishop of York in 665: presided over the great dedication ceremonies of St Peter's Church in Ripon seven years later, was banished from Northumbria in 678, appealed to Rome and went there for the second of his journeys. In 680 he was imprisoned and exiled: six years later he returned, in 691 was exiled for the second time and in 702 excommunicated and made a third journey to Rome. Finally, three years later he returned to Ripon and four years later died at Oundle and was buried at Ripon, a place which in his way he had loved so much and served so well. His shrine became a very considerable place of pilgrimage in the Middle Ages and the usual healing and miracles were associated with it.

His church and monastery at Ripon was destroyed by the Danes in the ninth century. A second church was demolished by the Normans as part of the Ravaging of the North. The Normans built a third church, which had as its patron Thomas of Bayeux, the first Norman Archbishop of York. The fourth church was inspired by Archbishop Roger Pont l'Evêque, the prelate who is notable for having supported Henry II in his quarrel with Thomas Becket of Canterbury. Another archbishop, Walter de Gray of York, built the present Early English West front, with its curiously truncated towers, the result of the dismantling in 1664 following the collapse of the central tower in 1660.

St Wilfrid's shrine, for so long a popular place of pilgrimage, went the way of all its kind at the Dissolution of the Monasteries, being dismantled and totally scattered. Ripon became a cathedral, the seat of a bishop, in 1836 with the foundation of the new diocese of Ripon. Today it is a cathedral and a parish church combined and, after all its stormy history, is a quiet and welcoming place for the pilgrim who likes to sit and think about the changes and chances of human life and history. But it is that strange crypt, or storeroom for relics, which impresses most and which brings us nearest of all to that Saxon, son of a thane, who travelled to Rome, was captivated by its splendours, and who did as much as any to champion its cause in the rough northern lands of his birth.

Lastingham, the monastery in a hidden place

'High and remote hills, which seem more suitable for the dens of robbers and haunts of wild beasts than for human habitation.' That was how Bede described the site which St Cedd, one of those English youths trained at Lindisfarne in the tradition of Celtic Christianity, chose as the site of the monastery which he founded in the year 654. The robbers and wild beasts have disappeared; but the high and remote hills are still there. I have known and loved this place for many years. In the centre of the village is a delightful inn where today's pilgrim can stay and, in the quiet of late evening, hear the tinkle of the water of the sacred well which runs at the foot of the little hill between church and inn. I went there straight from Ripon, going through Thirsk along the A170 to Helmsley and Kirkbymoorside. The road to Lastingham turns left shortly after Kirkbymoorside, and leads up through Hutton le Hole into the high North Yorkshire Moors, the 'remote hills' of Bede.

Any pilgrimage here should lead straight to the church. In this church, just as at Ripon, steps lead down to a truly remarkable crypt. But before that is visited, it is best to get clear in the mind something of the story which brought this place into existence, and of the moving events which took place there. For here we are very near indeed to the Celtic Church and to some of those personalities we were thinking about in Ripon. So this is the story of how the monastery at Lastingham came into being.

As usual, Bede tells it well. Cedd was Bishop of the East Saxons; but often visited what Bede calls the province of the Northumbrians, to preach. Ethelwald, son of the famous

Oswold, was King at this time in Deira. It was he, moved by the reputation of Cedd's holiness, who asked him to accept a grant of land in order that he might found a monastery. It was Ethelwald's hope that he himself could then often come to pray at this place and where, eventually, he might be buried. So Cedd, consenting, chose the wild and secret place which became the monastery of Lastingham, first purifying the site from the taint of the crimes which the wild men of the hills had already committed there, by a period of prayer and fasting very much in the tradition of the Celtic Church in which he had been trained. But before this was over he was summoned back into the service of the King, and so compelled to leave the work of completion to a brother priest, Cynibil. Cedd continued to administer the affairs of this monastery for many years. Then, during a time of plague, when he had returned on a visit, he fell sick and died there. It says much for the affection in which he was held that, when news of his death reached his monastery among the East Saxons, thirty of the brethren, desiring to be with the body of their father in God, made their way across the wilderness to Lastingham and there every single one of them also died of the pestilence. Cedd was buried first in the open at Lastingham and later, when a stone church was built, at the south side of the altar.

The monastery of Lastingham was for a time a considerable establishment although, like anything similar of Celtic origin, was simple in organisation. There were three classes of monks: senior or elder brethren, occupying themselves with the services of the church or in copying manuscripts; working brethren, who did the manual work about the place and novices. After the Council of Whitby, this simple rule changed to that of St Benedict; but the simple holiness of these early men at Lastingham has left still something in the atmosphere of this place which catches the heart.

Cedd had a brother, Chad, to whom he bequeathed the care of the monastery at Lastingham. He was not there long because, in the long absence of Wilfrid, Bishop of York and Abbot of Ripon, on one of his journeys to Rome, he was called upon to take his place at York, and after that to be Bishop of Lichfield.

But it was during his time that a strange event took place which leads oddly enough back to Ely. One day a stranger, an elderly man, carrying in his hand an axe and an adze presented himself at the monastery at Lastingham. According to Bede he carried the tools of his trade, because he was a working man, to show that he was entering the monastery not for the sake of an idle life, as some do, but in order to work, and he demonstrated this in practice; for since he found himself less able to meditate on the scriptures with profit, he undertook a larger amount of manual labour. In short, recognising his reverence and devotion, the Bishop admitted him to his house among the Brethren; and whenever they were engaged in study, he used to busy himself in essential tasks out of doors.

This was none other than Ovin, who had been steward to Etheldreda at Ely and whose stone cross we saw in the cathedral there. No mention was made at Ely of the fact that this man, after the death of Etheldreda, had in this way decided to renounce the world, as Bede says, and to make his way alone, no doubt by forest tracts, far off to Lastingham. He is the very image of a simple and holy man, very Saxon, very devout and sincere. He was to accompany Chad to Lichfield and end his life there.

With all this in mind, it is time now to go down into this wonderful crypt at Lastingham. It is one of the few apsidal crypts in England and is claimed by some to be the only one of its kind complete with a chancel, a nave and two side aisles. This is a very holy place indeed, rough-hewn, utterly silent and for many years reached only through a trap-door. The stone altar is not only very ancient but it may well have been that at which St Chad himself celebrated the holy mysteries. Arranged about the floor are some very interesting stones, including the carved cross head, dating again from Chad's time, which is part of the largest pre-Norman monuments in England, dug up near the porch of the church in 1838. There is also a broken stone said to have been once part of an ancient portable altar. And the dread fact that the Danes, or Vikings, made their way here is shown by the crudely carved hog's back tombstone with a rough effigy upon it which bears all the marks of their work. There is a small mystery about this. The *Anglo-Saxon Chronicle* records that Northmen, coming out of what it calls 'Haerethaland', which would be Denmark, in 793 'lamentably destroyed God's Church at Lindisfarne through rapin and slaughter'. Almost certainly, something like this must have happened even to hidden-away Lastingham because there is no record of any activity there until 1078, when this crypt was built to house the sacred remains of St Cedd. What, therefore, is the meaning of this hog's back tombstone now on the floor of the crypt? Could it be that among these Vikings there could have been Christians and the custom of Christian burial? There is no answer; only the mystery. But the serpent and winged dragon among the very old wooden carvings here were certainly Viking emblems. Nothing has been touched here since 1088. The Dissolution, which pulled to the ground such places as the great abbeys of Fountains and Rievaulx near by, spared Lastingham, presumably because it was so poor and secret a place. So there it continues the same as ever, in silence and solitude.

Whitby and the abbey on the cliffs

Some idea of the seafaring nature of this breezy town can be had from noting the strange archway over the entrance to a cemetery on the left of the road, made of two immense whalebones, for Whitby was once a port from which the whalers set out for the Greenland fisheries.

The abbey, now admirably maintained by the Department of the Environment, stands high on the cliffs over the harbour, and was almost certainly built upon the site of a Roman signalling

station, one of many which were set up around the coasts towards the end of the Roman occupation to give warning of sea raiders. Roman coins have been found in the place and according to Bede it was known as 'The Bay of the Beacon'. Whitby, indeed, figures largely in Bede's history, and for three reasons: the Synod of Whitby, the personality of its abbess, Hilda, and the charming story of Caedmon, England's first vernacular poet.

The Synod took place during the Easter of 664. When I was in Whitby it was not long after that season, and, among the ruins of the abbey, the wind blew very cold from the north, giving some idea of what life must have been like in the Saxon monastery, let alone its successor. The buildings there now give little indication to the outward eye as to what the Saxon monastery must have looked like; but there are traces among the excavations which have been made here which give some idea. The place would be surrounded by an enclosure, similar to that which still exists at Iona. Within this enclosure would be the church of the monastery, or even several of them. St Augustine's Abbey at Canterbury, for instance, had three, Wilfred built two at Hexham. But these would be very small, and often had side chapels which served as places for burials or prayer. And, since Whitby was a double monastery, the sexes would be divided in the main church longitudinally, men to the south and women to the north of a central partition. Around these churches would be the cells of the inmates and some larger buildings such as refectory and guest-house. It would all, by later standards of Norman building, be very crude and rough, as became its Saxon origins.

But all this area would have been crowded and animated on that day in 664, just after Easter, when the Synod of Whitby was in session. King Oswy presided, for it was his responsibility to decide between the Roman and the Celtic elements of the English Church. The details, as we saw earlier, were the date of the celebration of Easter and certain other ecclesiastical matters. The principle involved was the choice between two traditions of the English Church, as between the Celtic and the Roman. Wilfrid of Ripon was the spokesman for the Roman party: Coleman spoke

The original Whitby Abbey, a Saxon 'double monastery', accommodating both men and women, and presided over by the famous Hilda, was built on the site of a former Roman signal station overlooking the sea. Caedmon, the first English vernacular poet, was a monk here. The present ruins are of a later date. (*Department of the Environment*) for those of Lindisfarne. Bede gives the debate at length; but the essence of it was contained in what Wilfrid had to say when the King, surrounded by his thanes and members of the monastery, commanded him to speak.

'Our Easter customs', said Wilfrid,

> are those that we have seen universally observed in Rome, where the blessed Apostles Peter and Paul lived, taught, suffered and are buried. We have also seen the same customs generally observed throughout Italy and Gaul when we travelled through these countries for study and prayer. Furthermore, we have learnt that Easter is observed by men of different nations and languages at one and the same time, in Africa, Asia, Egypt, Greece, and throughout the world wherever the Church of Christ has spread. The only people who stupidly contend against the whole are those Scots and their partners in obstinacy the Picts and Britons, who inhabit only a portion of these the two uttermost islands of the ocean.

They were impressive words. Coleman, a simpler man, had little to say in reply. And when Wilfrid claimed for the whole Church the precedence for one whom he called the 'Blessed Prince of the Apostles, to whom our Lord said: "Thou art Peter, and upon this rock I will build my Church" ', the King gave his verdict for the Roman party. It was, in effect, the end of the Celtic Church as an effective force. Coleman returned to the North and the tradition which he represented vanished with him into the mists.

Hilda, Abbess of Whitby, was a very remarkable woman. For the first part of her life she lived as a Saxon noblewoman; for her last thirty-three years she followed the monastic life, having received the faith at the same time as Edwin when he had been baptised through the preaching of Paulinus. According to custom, she had to renounce all that she possessed when she became a nun. She served as Abbess at a monastery at Hartlepool, as it now is, and also at another house near Tadcaster before coming to Whitby. There she made a tremendous reputation for the place as a centre of learning and holiness. Bede, inevitably, tells of miracles associated with her life, such as that, when she was an infant, her mother dreamt of discovering a valuable jewel which shone so brightly that all Britain was lit by its splendour. This dream, he says, was fulfilled in Hilda, whose life afforded such a shining example. He also records a miracle of her death, telling of how, when she had suffered a feverish illness for six years, she died joyfully one dawn. The following night a vision of her passing into Heaven came to various of the sisters living at monasteries some distance away. One of these 'opening her eyes, as she thought, she saw the roof open, and a great light pour in from above and flood the room. While she gazed into this light, she saw the soul of God's servant Hilda borne up to Heaven.'

Hilda was buried at Whitby. But according to the twelfth-century historian, William of Malmesbury, her remains, together with parts of those of St Aidan, were moved from Whitby and Lindisfarne to Glastonbury in later centuries. The Saxon monastery was destroyed by the Danes in 867. The ruins which stand there now, high on the cliffs, represent those of an important Benedictine House, which lasted until the Dissolution.

The beautiful story of Caedmon takes us back to the holy simplicities of the Celtic Church. Caedmon, to whom there is a memorial cross in the present-day churchyard at Whitby, was a herdsman on the farm of the monastery. One night, as he slept among the beasts he had a dream, in which it seemed to him that a man called upon him to sing a song. Caedmon said that, being a simple man, he could not sing, which was why he had left a feast then going on in the hall of the monastery in order to return to his stable. But, the messenger from God pressed him whereupon Caedmon asked, 'What should I sing about?' The answer was 'Sing about the creation of all things.' Caedmon began to do so, and, in his native tongue. And what he sang was this:

Praise we the Fashioner now of Heavens fabric,
The majesty of his might and his minds wisdom,
Work of the World-Warden, worker of all wonders,
How he the Lord of Glory everlasting,
Wrought first for the race of men Heaven as a rooftree,
Then made he Middle Earth to be their mansion.

In the morning he was taken before Hilda with a report of this gift which had been laid upon him. She directed, in much delight, that, because God had given such grace to Caedmon, he should enter the monastery as a brother and be instructed in sacred history. So Caedmon, memorising all that he learnt, in a memorable phrase of Bede's, 'like one of the clean animals

chewing the cud, turned it into such melodious verse that his delightful renderings turned his instructors into auditors'.

Celtic Christianity, from out of the heart of which such legends come, has vanished into the silence and the solitudes. But its heart in some places still beats strongly. To follow the trail of it through Yorkshire is, admittedly, to leave aside many other places of significance, such as the great abbeys of Rievaulx and Fountains. But these are from a later age, and somehow seem to have less to say to our materialistic age, than the gentle simplicities of the Celtic Church. That is why, on my journey, I went from Whitby far to the north, to pick up the same trail again.

'One night, as he slept among the beasts, he had a dream.' (Caedmon at Whitby.)

CHAPTER 4

Into Northumberland

Durham – St Cuthbert
Jarrow – the Venerable Bede
Lindisfarne, or Holy Island
Hexham

The wonderful story of St Cuthbert

Whichever way you arrive at Durham the first sight of the great cathedral is a memorable experience. The situation of that enormous mass of building is truly dramatic, high on a promontory which plunges down through woods at its westward end to the River Wear below. So much has happened here, so enormous is the history of the place, so rich in legend and tradition, that it is difficult indeed to realise that all this began long ago with the arrival among the woods of a party of monks who, having for many years been carrying the coffin of St Cuthbert to and fro all over the wilderness of northern England, sought for it a resting-place. The body within the coffin had already remained uncorrupt for nearly 300 years. An object of veneration then, it was to become, especially when placed within the great shrine within the cathedral which eventually arose in this place, the centre of a pilgrim cult second only in fame to that of St Thomas at Canterbury. And because St Cuthbert dead was the cause of so many marvels, and is the continuing centre of so much fame, it follows that little of this can be truly understood without also a knowledge of his life.

Durham Cathedral, for many centuries the great pilgrim centre of the North built around the relics of St Cuthbert, whose body finally came to rest here after many wanderings. The cathedral contains also the tomb of Bede. (*The British Tourist Authority*)

He is a most attractive figure. He seems, in a strange way, still to be around, still to be a living force. He was always loved, he was always revered, and to this day he is the Saint of the North beyond compare.

Even more striking is the fact that he seems, somehow, to be still alive. The cause could be the power of his personality, strong enough to overcome time. It could equally be a consequence of the very strange adventures which befell his body and which continued for centuries after his death, which, lengthily and lovingly recalled by Bede, took place on an island off Lindisfarne. Far from being allowed to rest in peace he was moved at least eight times between his death in 687 and his final and, as it turned out, sensational translation to his shrine in Durham Cathedral in 1104. There are, additionally, six occasions on record when his coffin was opened, the last one in 1889.

A famous story of this post-mortem power of Cuthbert involved no less a person than William the Conqueror himself. Calling at Durham in 1072 he demanded to see the Saint's body, on pain of instant execution for the monks should they fail to produce it. Terrified, and fearful both of the command and the sacrilege involved in obeying it, they prayed to Cuthbert. The Conqueror, immediately smitten with a painful disorder, fled the church where he was attending Mass, and did not stop until he had reached the Tees.

Yet Cuthbert, so strongly intervening from the grave in human affairs was a person who in his life sought solitude, and went to great lengths to obtain it. He was born about 635 near Melrose Abbey not more than two centuries after the Roman withdrawal, when the Saxon Conquest was not yet complete, or the invaders wholly Christianised. Nothing is known of Cuthbert's parents, though his character suggests princely stock. Among the mass of legends about him is at least one which tells how, from youth, he was attracted to the religious life. Tending his sheep one night on the Lammermuir Hills he had a vision of a great light in the sky, heard music, saw angels bearing a soul to Heaven. The next day he learnt that in the night Aidan, the monk from Iona who had converted the wild Northumbrians, and become Bishop of Lindisfarne, had died. That vision had lasting effects on Cuthbert. The next day he left his shepherding and, a tall and rangy young man, carrying his spear, rode to Melrose Abbey and asked for admission. Boisil, a monk renowned for holiness, who was to become a mentor and beloved companion of Cuthbert, seeing him approach said, in words evocative of Scripture, 'Behold the servant of the Lord.' And when Eata the Abbot returned, Cuthbert was received.

Some lovely stories are attached to him, some strongly recalling the characteristic features of Celtic Christianity: the love of its followers for solitude, for off-shore islands with no sound but the beat of waves and the cry of birds, and also a curious *rapprochement* with animals. Here is one. Cuthbert was staying at Coldingham, a double monastery where Ebba was Abbess and where, indeed, Etheldreda of Ely spent some time. He was there to preach to the nuns, on one of his many missionary journeys. A monk, noticing that Cuthbert was out all night, on one occasion secretly followed him to see what happened. He beheld him under the moonlight walking into the sea on the lonely beach. There he stood all night, praising God until dawn. When he emerged on to the sands, two seals came to wipe his feet and to breathe on him, waiting afterwards to receive his blessing. The incident became a favourite subject with manuscript illustrations of Cuthbert's life.

When Eata went to be Prior at Ripon he took Cuthbert with him. But the outcome of the Synod of Whitby and of the powerful intervention of Wilfrid caused Cuthbert to withdraw with his abbot back to Melrose and then, Eata having become Bishop of Lindisfarne, to that island which was for ever afterwards to be associated with his name. Here Cuthbert, though himself inwardly preferring the old Celtic ways, was yet loyal to the decisions made at Whitby, and urged the monks at Lindisfarne, some of whom were still hostile, to be reconciled to the new ways. In these years he travelled greatly on missionary journeys over the wild country of the North, mostly on foot, in all weathers, across moors, through forests, taking the Gospel to primitive people.

Numerous are the legends of Cuthbert in this period of his missionary journeys: how he extinguished a fire which the Devil had caused in order to draw folk away from his preaching, how he healed the sick, was miraculously fed in the wilderness by a fish which an eagle had dropped on the river bank.

After some years of this hard life, Cuthbert felt a strong urge for solitude. So he withdrew, first to a lonely cell on Lindisfarne itself and then, finding even this isolation insufficient, to a tiny outpost of the Farne Islands, seawards of Lindisfarne, a few miles off Bamburgh. Here he dug a cell downwards into the rock,

roii erant aduisendu̅ · & paup̅tate pariȶ 35
ac rusticitate sua doctoɽ p̅hibebant acces̄
siu̅ · Quos̄ tam̅ ille pio libent̅ mancipat̄
laboȓ tanta doctrine excolebat industria:
uȶ de monasterio egrediens̄ sepe ebdomada
integra aliq̅n̅do duab; ut tr̅ib; · n̅ nunqua̅
etia̅ m̅se pleno domu̅ n̅ redirec:s̄ demoraȶ
in montani⸱plebe̅ rustica̅ uerbo p̅dicati
on̅is simul & exe̅plo uirtutis̄ ad celestia uocare.
X.º in a̅ialia marı̅s inq̅ p̅n̅or oȓauerat illi egresso
p̅buerint obseq̅ȗ · & fr̅q̅ hec uiderat p̅timore'
languescens̄ eius̄ sic oȓatione recreatus ;

Cuo̅ ȣero scs̄ uiȓ in eode̅ monasterio
uirtutib; signisq; succrescereȶ · famaq;

Sea creatures, probably seals, lick the feet of St Cuthbert after he had spent a night praying by the sea-shore at Lindisfarne, observed by the monk who is watching on the left. (*The Masters and Fellows of University College, Oxford*) surrounding it with a low wall covered with a primitive roof which meant that, when he was within, his only view was the sky. Near by he built an oratory and guest-house, for even here, on this rocky islet, so great was his fame that people came seeking him.

But he was not to be left long undisturbed. There is a pre-Raphaelite painting in the church on Lindisfarne which shows a king, Egfrid of Northumbria, and an archbishop, Theodore of Canterbury, pressing a crosier on Cuthbert, who is working on his plot of land on the islet. A nice detail in this picture is the pair of crows, representing yet another Cuthbert legend, to the effect that these creatures, more probably ravens or jackdaws, had once pestered him by pulling out the thatch of his shelter for their nests. First he asked them to stop: then he banished them from the island. A little later these two came back, trailing their wings and drooping their heads, croaking for pardon.

But now, for a while, this simple life was over. King and Archbishop had come to beg Cuthbert to accept the bishopric of Hexham. He refused at first, but at last gave way on condition that, if he had to be a bishop, it must be of Lindisfarne and Lindisfarne only. Eata, already holding that position, consequently resigned it and went to Hexham. Cuthbert, after a winter of prayer and meditation on his island, was consecrated the following Easter.

There now began another period of arduous missionary journeys throughout the North. Again the same scenes were repeated as on his earlier journeys; the people from wild hill settlements coming out to meet him, the Bishop preaching, baptising, confirming and healing. Yet Cuthbert now fifty-two years old, must have known that he had not long to live. Once at Carlisle, encountering an old friend, a monk called Herbert, he told him that they would never again meet on this earth. To the heartbroken man he promised that, as indeed came to pass, they would die at the same time. For Cuthbert that day was near. After the Christmas of 686, he resigned his see and, returning to his island hermitage, awaited the end. As he entered the boat one of the brethren said to him, 'Tell us, my Lord Bishop, when we may hope for your return?' Cuthbert answered: 'When you bring my body back here.' He died on 20 March 687.

Now began the long-continued wanderings of this sacred corpse. They buried Cuthbert on Lindisfarne in a stone sarcophagus on the right side of the altar. Miracles and healings at once began, taking the usual forms. An insane youth was cured by a particle of earth which had mingled with the water in which the body had been washed. Sick people were healed at the place where the same water had been poured away. The greatest miracle of all, reminiscent among other saints, of Etheldreda of Ely, was that, eleven years after his burial, when the monks opened the coffin in order to place it in a better situation for veneration, they found the body uncorrupt. This miracle laid the foundations of centuries of veneration of Cuthbert. Some say that the uncorrupt body was a miracle; others that the body had been embalmed, yet others that the dry sand of Lindisfarne had preserved the corpse in a mummified state. Whatever the cause, Cuthbert's body had now been moved once.

The second movement of it followed the arrival of a Danish raiding party who landed on Lindisfarne in 793 and wrecked the church. The following year they returned, this time causing the monks to flee, taking the body with them. They also took along some bones of St Aidan, and of Bishop Eata and the head of King Oswald. Their wanderings with this burden, over moors, along valleys, through woods and across mountains continued a long time, the coffin on a bier, only seven of the monks, and those most renowned for holiness, being permitted to touch it. After many wanderings, the party decided to cross over to Ireland. But, as they left the beach a storm came up, driving them back to shore again. In the tumult a very precious document, the Lindisfarne Gospel, was washed overboard. Legend has it that the monks sought desperately all along the western coasts for this object until eventually they found it stranded on the sands at a place called Withern in Galway. Legend it may be. The hard fact is that this very document, in the British Museum now, has on its pages the stains of sea water.

As the party went its way, increasing the piety of the people as it passed by, it gathered many gifts of land and treasure in honour of the Saint, which did much to lay the foundations of the later great wealth of Durham Cathedral. After the failure of the attempt to cross to Ireland, the party with the body, travelled to Craike in Yorkshire. There it was revealed to the Abbot in a vision of St Cuthbert, that the Saint ordered him to go to the Danes and to suggest that one of their number, Guthred, should be brought back from slavery, into which he had been sold, and made King of Northumbria. This was agreed: the new King, by way of

'Eventually they found it stranded on the sands.' (The Lindisfarne Gospels which had been lost by monks.)

reward, settled Cuthbert's monks at an old Roman station at Chester-le-Street, where a shrine was created for Cuthbert. This, then, was the third move which the body sustained, and here it remained for 110 years, constantly gathering fame and wealth: copies of the Gospels, ornaments, vessels in silver and gold, robes, jewellery, money. I saw a stole, the gift of King Athelstan, in the fascinating Durham Cathedral Treasury, a place which today's pilgrim should on no account miss. When I made this journey I visited Chester-le-Street but, alas, found scarcely anything of these 110 years when Cuthbert's shrine was there.

Now the fourth movement of the body was impending. Again the Danes invaded, this time in 995, whereupon the monks at Chester-le-Street, took the body to Ripon for security until the danger passed. After a short time there, turning north again, they came to a place where the cart upon which the body was carried, became stuck in the mire. Three days of fasting and prayer followed in which the advice of Cuthbert was sought. He revealed that he wished his shrine to be in a place called the Dunholme. But no one knew where it was until, according to the famous story, some of the monks overheard two women speaking about a lost cow which was said to have strayed into 'the Dunholme'. Investigated, this turned out to be a wooded promontory in a loop of the River Wear, which is where Durham Cathedral stands now.

So the monks, making a rude shelter, placed the coffin there till they could construct a wooden church, which survived for three years during which time people from far and wide came in not only to venerate the miracle-working corpse, which had been wandering for 300 years, but also to help in building a stone cathedral to contain its shrine.

This is the point at which a curious character called Elfred Westou, enters the story. As the Sacrist, he was the chief custodian of the coffin, enjoying the privilege of opening it whenever he wished. He would change the clothing of it quite frequently, would exhibit trimmings from Cuthbert's nails and hair which according to him, had always continued to grow. A large ivory comb was kept in the coffin and found there when, centuries later at the Dissolution, it was opened. This Elfred also developed the habit of collecting relics whenever possible and placing them in the coffin. It was in this way that the bones of Bede himself found their way here, as it seems clear that Elfred must have stolen them when visiting Jarrow on the customary anniversary of Bede's death, when the bones were exhibited. That ivory liturgical comb can be seen to this day in the treasury at Durham.

The sixth movement of the body was now impending. The Norman Conquest had taken place; there were tumults in the North which the Conqueror himself resolved to put down, just as happened at York and elsewhere. In the face of this threat the monks in charge of Cuthbert decided to flee to Lindisfarne. But the tide was in when they reached the shore and there seemed no way across. They did not know that the island is separated from the mainland every day in this manner, so that it seemed a miracle when, the waters falling back, they found a way open before them.

They returned to Durham in 1070, the seventh movement of the body. The eighth, and final one, took place in 1104 when Cuthbert was moved into the splendid shrine which he was to occupy throughout the long years of his cult in the Middle Ages. The occasion was dramatic. Among the large and distinguished company, there arose doubts as to whether the body within the coffin was, after all this time and so many wanderings, genuine. It was decided to open it. Approaching this task in understandable trepidation, the clergy waited in the cathedral until nightfall. They then removed the lid. Beneath were revealed two more coffins, one inside the other, the carving on the inner one exactly agreeing with Bede's description of it written 400 years before. When the lid of this was raised they found first a shelf, on which lay a copy of the Gospels, Cuthbert's small silver portable altar, and a collection of bones placed there by that inveterate relic hunter Elfred Westou. They then removed the wrappings on the body. It was found to be uncorrupt, complete and even flexible, so that there was some difficulty in lifting it out and laying it on the floor near by while the coffin was cleared. It was now almost dawn, and so they replaced it. The following night it was again removed, examined and returned to its coffin.

But the matter was not yet finished. The news of this discovery roused the suspicions of some of the prelates assembled. One of them, strongly objecting to what had been done, felt that it should have taken place in the presence of the whole company, or at any rate of authorised representatives of it. So, once again, the coffin was opened, this time in the presence, among others, of four visiting abbots, Alexander, the King of Scotland's brother and a large company of monks and secular clergy. One of the company, the Abbot of Seez, being the only one permitted to touch the sacred body, did so thoroughly, lifting up the head, testing the joints, even twisting the ears backwards and forwards. This time there was no doubt: St Cuthbert was pronounced truly dead, but with his body whole and uncorrupt. It was then, among many miraculous manifestations and much ceremony, placed in its shrine.

Today's pilgrim to Durham, looking up that stone slab in the cathedral with the word 'Cuthbertus' upon it and little ornament but the four candles placed at each corner, can too easily miss the power and the glory which this famous shrine possessed in the Middle Ages. The great cathedral had grown around it. Behind the high altar, where the relics were kept and in the centre of which stood the shrine, it was said that there were to be found 'the most sumptuous and richest jewels in all the land . . . for great was the gifts and godly devotions of Kings and Queens and other estates at that time towards God and St Cuthbert in that church'. All sorts of men and women made the pilgrimage there and, in the customary manner, sought inspiration, relief and healing as well as the purging of offences committed. The shrine was the source of great wealth. The relics, accumulated around the shrine, became famous, and give a vivid picture of what such a cult really meant. There was an elbow of St Christopher, a finger of St Lawrence, some of the hair of St Ambrose. There were griffins' eggs, a piece of John the Baptist's shirt, a vessel containing some of the Virgin's milk, a piece of St Andrew's cross a piece of the rock from which Christ ascended, a thorn from his crown, some of the hair of saints with skin attached. Additionally, there were rich gifts such as cups, crosses, caskets of silver and ivory and gold and precious stones. And to the enormous assortment of relics and treasures was added, after the Battle of Neville's Cross outside Durham, a purported piece of the true Cross, captured along with the King of Scotland. Also, like the shrine of St Alban, there was a wooden cover which was raised whenever the Saint's body was to be venerated. Attached to the rope were six silver bells, so that the tinkle of these would echo through the enormous building whenever a veneration impended.

A tradition about St Cuthbert, which seems out of character, is that he had an abhorrence of women. But it is certainly a fact that a line of blue marble inserted into the floor at the western end of the nave is said to have represented the point beyond which

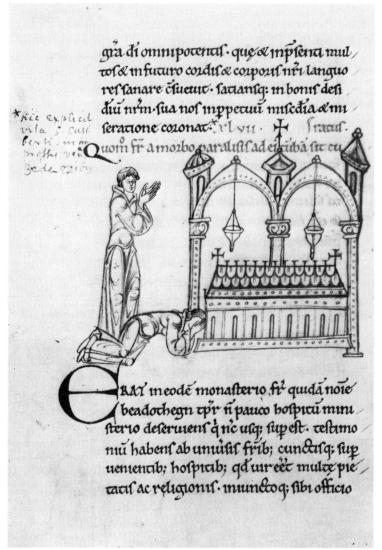

St Cuthbert's Shrine in Durham, as shown on a 12th century manuscript of Bede's Life of Cuthbert. Monks pray before it. The lid would be raised and bells rung whenever a veneration was to take place. (*The Masters and Fellows of University College, Oxford*)

women could not pass. Thus, when Queen Philippa came to Durham with Edward III and was discovered sleeping with her husband in the priory, she was told by the monks to leave immediately, even though it was the middle of the night. Even as late as the fifteenth century two Newcastle women, who dressed up as men and entered the forbidden zone, were, being caught, compelled to show themselves to the indignant public still wearing the clothes of their masquerade.

When the end came for this famous shrine strange events took place as Cuthbert was disturbed. The official commissioners who arrived to begin the work were Doctor Leigh, Doctor Henley and Mr Blythman. Obviously, their first task was to strip the shrine of its treasures. They then gave orders that the marble tomb should be broken open, which revealed the coffin inside, bound with iron. To break into it required a sledge-hammer, not a very easy implement to use by a man standing on a ladder. However, the coffin was eventually opened and revealed a complete body clothed in mass vestments, something rather like a crosier lying beside it, and, astonishingly, a face only lightly bearded. In the breaking open of the coffin this workman accidentally broke one of the legs and called down to the experts standing below that he had done so. Doctor Henley then commanded him to throw down the bones. The man replied that this was impossible, because the body was entire. Doctor Leigh, going up to see for himself, was sufficiently astonished to call up his colleague, Henley. Both then saw, and recorded that the body was indeed entire, and that the clothing in which it was wrapped was unstained. So it was removed and buried under the blue marble slab, on the exact site of the former shrine, where indeed it still is. All this took place in 1542.

But Cuthbert was not even yet to be left in peace. On 17 May 1827 the slab, in the presence of various cathedral authorities, and under the supervision of James Raine, Librarian to the Dean and Chapter, was raised. The object seems to have been to disprove the legend that somehow, during the time of Mary Tudor, the body had been removed and buried secretly in a place known only to senior clergy of the Benedictine Order, who passed on the secret, generation after generation. Raine and his superiors may also, and more probably, have been motivated by general curiosity. At any rate the legend was disproved. Cuthbert was still there. Beneath the slab was soil: beneath that another stone, and beneath that again a large pit about 5 feet deep, lined with stone.

'She was told by the monks to leave immediately.' (Queen Philippa at Durham.)

St Cuthbert's 7th century Pectoral Cross, worn by him as a Bishop and discovered in his coffin. It can now be seen in the cathedral exhibition. (*Dean and Chapter of Durham Cathedral*)

At the very bottom of this excavation was a large oak coffin, much decayed. Beneath this was another, also decayed. In this were discovered a collection of human bones which were assumed to be some of the relics which had once existed around the shrine. The removal of these revealed a third coffin, bearing marks which identified it as that which had been made to hold the body at the great translation of 1104. Inside was a skeleton wrapped in cloth which turned out to be an outer sheet of linen, covering still further wrappings. It also contained an ivory comb.

Also revealed was a pectoral cross of gold and cloisonne work which, worn in life by Cuthbert himself had been reverently buried with him in 687. This, together with much else, may now be seen in the Durham Cathedral Treasury. For me, to stand and gaze upon this small and beautiful cross, which has survived so much was a most moving experience.

Incredibly, Cuthbert's grave was opened yet again, this time in 1899, apparently in order that an anatomist should have opportunity of examining the bones. He reported the skeleton to be that of a muscular man with a left shin-bone missing, which would be the injury done by the workman who had opened the coffin for those three commissioners who had arrived to dismantle the shrine in 1542. This time the bones were replaced for good, and the grave was sealed. There is no longer the tinkle of bells as a cover is raised from a shrine above it. Even so, thousands upon thousands of people still make their pilgrimage to that bare slab, and think their own thoughts, as they look upon the single word which it bears 'Cuthbertus'.

The cathedral is immensely impressive, towering upon its hill alongside the castle. Sir Walter Scott wrote:

Grey towers of Durham
Yet well I love thy mixed and massive piles.
Half church of God, half castle 'gainst the Scot;
And long to roam these venerable aisles,
With records stored of deeds long since forgot.

Here also lie the bones of Bede, of whom there is much more to discover, and that recently revealed, at Jarrow. But here he rests in Durham because that strange character, Elfred Westou, filched his bones from Jarrow and placed them with Cuthbert. Later they were set apart in a special shrine of their own, which would be carried in procession round the cathedral on Ascension Day, Whit Sunday and Trinity Sunday. James Raine, who opened the grave of Cuthbert in 1827, examined this one also in 1830 and, found in a place where the right hand would have been if raised in blessing, an iron finger-ring plated with gold. This, now in the Cathedral Museum, may well have been worn by Bede himself.

But whatever splendours catch the eye, and whatever history stirs the heart in Durham Cathedral, the great truth for the pilgrim always to remember is that everything sprang from Cuthbert, his name and fame. Therefore it may truly be said, as was once remarked of Wren, the architect of St Paul's, 'Si monumentum requiris, circumspice' (if you wish to see his monument, look around you).

There is one relic of Cuthbert which would have particularly pleased him. Most great Christian establishments in the Middle Ages had the right of offering sanctuary to the fugitive. By this, any offender fleeing from justice or, equally as often, injustice and private vengeance, was safe so long as he could come under the protection of the Church. St Cuthbert's sanctuary at Durham became one of the most famous in the country, a fame which arose from his dying words, spoken to his monks when he understood that they would wish to take his body to the mainland. He said, 'I think it better for you that I should remain here, on account of the fugitive and criminals who may flee to my corpse for refuge; and when they have thus obtained an asylum, in as much as I have enjoyed the fame, humble though I am, of being a servant of Christ, you may think it necessary to intercede for such before the secular rulers. . . .' So the sanctuary knocker, reproduced in its thousands as a tourist curiosity, still hangs on the cathedral's North door. A fugitive only had to reach it and bang on the door to be let in, to escape the terrors pursuing him. A bell would ring to give notice that a man had taken sanctuary: a monk would run to let him in, and he would be taken to the Prior and questioned as to his crime, given lodging for thirty-seven days, after which he would have to go before a coroner, confess his crime and, conducted to the coast by a civil officer, leave the country for ever. An ancient document, *The Sanctuarium Bunelmense* records an actual case. A man imprisoned for theft escaped and found sanctuary. Being admitted, he took his stand before the shrine of Cuthbert and refused to be moved. When, before the Coroner, he had undertaken to leave the country, he stripped and assumed the cloak of St Cuthbert, a black gown with a yellow cross on the shoulder. He then set off for the coast, to be seen no more. Could anything speak more eloquently of the love which even the name of Cuthbert could arouse, and the security which the strength of his saintly reputation could impart?

The sanctuary knocker at Durham. Anyone fleeing from justice, or from the pursuit of his enemies and seeking the sanctuary of the church, could not be touched provided he had laid hold of the ring beneath the knocker. He would then be admitted and his case heard. (*Dean and Chapter of Durham Cathedral*)

Bede, and new treasures at Jarrow

In the monastery of St Paul at Jarrow, Bede spent most of his life, and because he is the source of most of what we can discover of the saints of Anglo-Saxon England, it is important to know more of him, too. Recently an archaeological investigation has been completed by Professor Rosemary Cramp of Durham University into the origins of Bede's Jarrow, and indeed of the whole culture of which he was a part, which reveals much about him. The results are to be seen in St Paul's Church, and in Jarrow Hall near by, which now contains the Bede Monastery Museum, where one of Professor Cramp's most exciting discoveries is to be found, the oldest stained glass in Western Christendom, made by craftsmen imported from Gaul when St Paul's was built between 681 and 685.

To the south of the church lie the site of the remains of the Saxon and later Norman monasteries. This, a place of pilgrimage for many, is of great importance for the whole Christian story in England. It contains, among other things, the most complete layout of a Saxon monastery in the country. The whole place is a reminder of the fact that 1,300 years ago Jarrow was famous throughout Europe: the monastery of St Paul a centre of scholarship and art, the books of Bede read in every Christian country. A journey to St Paul's Church and to Jarrow Hall nearby is, therefore, a rewarding way to relive and appreciate the splendour and excitement of this part of our past.

But who was Bede? Like Cuthbert of Durham he entered the monastic life as a boy, being brought by his parents to what was then the new monastery at Monkwearmouth. This would be around the year 680, not more than a century and a half after the arrival of the Saxons. He was therefore near in time to St Aidan, the missionary Bishop who had come from Iona to convert the wild people of the North. From him Bede gathered the tradition of simple holiness which was always a part of his own life. He was influenced intellectually by another of the great men of the Saxon Church, Benedict Biscop, a man who, devoted to the development of learning, made many journeys to Rome and brought back from there books and other apparatus of culture. It was Biscop who built the monastery at Monkwearmouth which Bede entered. Not long afterwards a companion house, a few miles away at Jarrow, was founded, where a monk named Ceolfrith was placed in charge. It was he who took Bede, who

An interesting model of a Saxon Monastery in Jarrow Hall. In such a place as this Bede would have spent his life. Monasteries of a later, Norman age would have been much more elaborate. (*The Bede Monastery Museum*)

grew up under his rule at Jarrow and remained in that monastery for the rest of his long life.

Bede, a man of great holiness, was also a man of great learning. St John of Beverley, sometime Bishop of Hexham, was one of his mentors in the priesthood. But his general learning was immense: Latin he knew intimately; Greek he could have learned from Benedict Biscop. He knew some Hebrew, he had read widely in the works of such fathers of the Church as Ambrose, Jerome, Augustine and Gregory the Great. He loved and knew his own native Anglo-Saxon poetry, in that tongue which the herdsman Caedmon at Whitby had used. And, as Caedmon has been called the father of English poetry, so Bede has been called the father of English history. Men far afield in Europe were glad to help him with information and books. Some of those of whom he wrote he had known personally. And yet he was a very humble man. Of himself he wrote: 'I gave all my thoughts to meditating upon the Scriptures, and in the intervals of the monastic round and the daily care of chanting in the church, my sweetest delight was ever in learning or teaching or writing.'

Stories were told about him just as he had told stories of so

105

many others. One concerned the time when a 'great pestilence' had killed off all the monks at Jarrow except the boy Bede and his abbot, Ceolfrith. These two were left to carry on the daily round of services in the empty church. Alcuin of York told of how Bede used often to say: 'I know that the angels visit the canonical hours and the assemblies of the Brethren. What if they do not find me in the congregation? Would they not say, "Where is Bede?"'

Another story was of his death. He continued writing and teaching to the end, suffering from increasing breathlessness, and in the afternoon of his last day he shared out his few small personal treasures among his brethren. In the evening one of the young monks to whom he had been dictating said that there was yet one sentence to write in the translation into Anglo-Saxon of a part of St John's Gospel upon which he had been working. Bede dictated it and then lay back saying, 'Good, it is finished.' There is another story about how he came by his title. When a monk was trying to write his epitaph he could not find a suitable adjective to describe the man, so he left his page blank overnight. When he returned to it in the morning he found that an angelic hand had written in the word 'venerabilis' – venerable. It is a great thing now to be able, in St Paul's Church at Jarrow, to visit the place in which this very man worshipped.

But the glories of Jarrow were to be short-lived. Here, as elsewhere, the Vikings struck hard, in 793 attacking the place, one year after they had descended upon Lindisfarne. For 200 years afterwards there was little life there. But of Bede it could be said that, 'he being dead, yet speaketh'. There was a monk, Aldwin, Prior of Winchcombe in Gloucestershire, who was so moved by reading Bede's history, that he undertook an expedition, joined by two monks from Evesham, to visit ruined monastic sites in the North, by that time destroyed not only by the Vikings but also by the scorched earth policy of William the Conqueror.

The picture of these three, one of whom had actually been a soldier in William's army, making their way through the forests on foot, with a packhorse carrying their books and vestments, kindles the imagination. They went to Whitby and eventually found their way to Jarrow, repairing, as far as they were able, the sacred sites as they went. Eventually, after many changes and chances, a Benedictine community, a cell of Durham, was established at Jarrow and assumed considerable importance until, like so much else, it was swept away at the Reformation.

Island of the saints

On the morning when I reached Lindisfarne, on a bright day of big skies and sailing cloud, the road was still wet from the outgoing tide and the cars which had been waiting to cross were just beginning to move. The route to Holy Island is easier than it used to be; but there is still a Pilgrim's Way across the sands marked with poles and provided with refuge boxes for those caught by the tide. This is not only a relic of the past. Thousands, as pilgrims, use this way every year. The whole area is one of great interest. Bamburgh Castle, some few miles south, was where the kings of Northumbria were crowned. Off the coast are the Farne Islands, which can be reached from Seahouses, and which are a breeding ground for seals and a bird sanctuary and the abode of the eider-duck, commonly and charmingly known

Memorial to St Aidan on Holy Island. Lindisfarne Castle is in the distance.
(*Reproduced by kind permission of Bamforth & Co. Ltd., Holmfirth, Yorkshire*)

as 'St Cuthbert's chicks'. The castle on Holy Island itself dates from the sixteenth century, and owes its existence to the need for defence against the Scots, just as does the much older Bamburgh. There is a very fine view from the upper platform of this castle northwards to the Cheviot Hills, and St Abb's Head where Etheldreda of Ely, who keeps appearing in this story, once took refuge from her husband, a scene depicted in the carving on one of the pillars in Ely Cathedral.

But Aidan and Cuthbert are the evocative names for the pilgrim to Lindisfarne. There is now nothing surviving of the monastery which they knew. But there are handsome ruins of the later priory, which have a wonderful atmosphere. On the day I was there the ancient parish church of St Mary soon filled with school-children, brought over the causeway by coach, and it was good to see them marvelling at the tale told them by the parish priest as he spoke of Aidan and Cuthbert and all those saints of old. But for me the greatest attraction on Lindisfarne is the Priory Museum.

A remarkable thing here is a round-headed tombstone with, on one side, a carving of armed Northumbrians with swords and battle-axes and, on the other side, two figures kneeling before the cross with sun and moon above. It is said that this strange object depicts the Northumbrians before and after their conversion to Christianity, and the sun and the moon demonstrate how pagan ideas could be and were incorporated into Christianity. Here also is a collection of 'pillow stones', once thought to have been placed beneath the heads of corpses, but actually objects which were laid flat on the surface of the grave. It is unusual that on one of these a woman's name, Osgyth, is inscribed, suggestive of the possibility that the community at Lindisfarne included women, not as members of a mixed monastery of the Whitby kind, but as wives or daughters of the clergy.

However, the greatest treasure produced by this early community is not here but in the British Museum, the Lindisfarne Gospels, a book made up of the four Gospels, copied from the version of St Jerome, and two epistles, the whole written on pages of vellum with beautiful illumination. This was the book lost at sea for a while by those monks fleeing with the body of Cuthbert.

This takes us to the story of the death of that saint. He was on his lonely island retreat when his final illness came upon him. Bede had the details of what happened from the then Abbot of

The figure of St Luke from the Lindisfarne Gospels. This famous document, now in the British Museum, was written by Bishop Eadfride about 700 in honour of St Cuthbert. This was the Gospel which the monks carried with them as they bore the body of the saint on its long wanderings over the north of England. (*The British Library*)

Lindisfarne, Herefrith, who had been with Cuthbert on the island and seeing how ill his master was, begged him to return to the mainland. Yet Cuthbert refused, although some of the monks were allowed to cross over to look after the dying Bishop. His last words to those gathered about him were that they should continue to live in peace, as he had always bid them do. When he died two torches were waved as a signal across to Lindisfarne in the dark of the winter morning. Then the body, wrapped in waxed cloth, was ferried across to Lindisfarne, and from that point began its wanderings.

This island of saints, Lindisfarne, is a very sacred and evocative place. It has been said that every pilgrim in England should visit Canterbury. It could surely be said with equal truth that every pilgrim should visit Holy Island.

The abbey at Hexham

I came to this splendid little town in mid-afternoon, in time for a leisurely tour of St Andrew's Abbey before the red-cassocked choir came down the night stair, by which in centuries past the monks used to come to sing their office. Nearby is an impressive memorial to an age long before. Vividly sculptured, it depicts a mounted Roman officer and, on the ground beneath the horse, thrusting savagely upwards into it, a figure of a savage. It is a memorial to a young Roman tribune, possibly a scion of a noble family who, sent to do his military service at this outpost of Empire, died on some cavalry foray into the wild land north of the Wall. Nor is this the only echo of Rome in this abbey. Beneath the present church is a Saxon crypt. One of the stones making a part of a doorway at the far end of it was once used as an altar to Apollo Maponus.

St Wilfrid, that busy and turbulent character who had so much to do with Ripon, as Bishop of Hexham created this abbey church. His builders, when they began in 674, brought stone from the Roman camp at the present-day Corbridge. Thus are these striking memories of Rome embedded in the very heart of the church. It was the relics which, just as at Ripon, Wilfrid brought back from Rome and placed in a relic chamber at the far

'Two torches were waved as a signal across to Lindisfarne.' (Death of Cuthbert.)

end of the crypt, that brought pilgrims here. Again as at Ripon, they went down a narrow stair, peered into the shrine with its mysterious objects of veneration and returned up a further stairway into the nave. There in the dimness, illuminated only by lamps formed of stone bowls with a wick burning in oil, pilgrims who had made their way across formidable country, came to worship. The modern pilgrim may well find his imagination stirred – I certainly did – not only by this place but equally by the Roman stones, by the Roman altar and particularly by the Roman memorial to the young tribune, all speaking as loudly as a trumpet call of those long past days of the legions.

Above this crypt, in the choir of the abbey, stands a carved stone seat known sometimes as St Wilfrid's Chair, or, more accurately, as the Fridstol. There was a very similar object to be found in Beverley Minster. Both are seats of sanctuary.

But Hexham Abbey, or so it seemed to me on that afternoon, was particularly suitable a place at which to say a farewell to some of these saintly men and women who were once part of the Christian heritage of Northumbria, and who have deeply affected the Christian history of this whole island. Some of them figure again in the pilgrim story of the Midlands, where next I went.

CHAPTER 5

Through the Midlands to Malmesbury

Repton – St Wystan
Lichfield – St Chad
Worcester – St Oswald and St Wulstan
Hereford – St Ethelbert and St Thomas Cantilupe
Hailes – The Holy Blood
Gloucester – Edward II
Malmesbury – St Aldhelm

A strange crypt at Repton

One day in the year 1779 a workman digging a grave in the chancel of the church at Repton fell through the floor, to find himself in a large chamber, the very existence of which had been forgotten all through the eighteenth century and probably before. Thus was revealed, at least in part, an ancient crypt of much interest to the pilgrim story in England and a fascinating place to visit now. There it lies in the quiet of Repton village, halfway between Derby and Burton-upon-Trent in the rolling Midlands countryside. When I last was there on a grey day, it was just possible, down in the crypt, to hear the voices of boys on the playing-fields of the public school which dominates the place. Up above, in the interesting church, there were memorials to headmasters: but down below in this crypt were silent evidences to another age altogether.

It is evident at a glance that this is no ordinary crypt; but something else as well. And this is true. The *Anglo-Saxon Chronicle* records that King Ethelbald of Mercia, having been murdered nearby in 757 was buried at Repton, almost certainly here. The historian Florence of Worcester says that another king of Mercia, Wiglaf, was also interred in the mausoleum which he had built for himself. This would be around the year 840. It would have been in the years previous to this, when the mausoleum was being created, that the pilasters and twisted columns, so striking a feature now, were set up within this crypt. So here already is evidence that this Midlands village was once a centre of some importance.

But there is a strange feature yet to be accounted for: stone steps have been cut at some later date down into this burial-place. Today's visitor, in fact, enters the crypt by steps leading down from the north side of the chancel, and these steps are very worn, and the passageway they follow has obviously been cut through the walls of the original mausoleum. For me, steps worn in this way have an immediate fascination. Whose were the feet that, for a long time and in considerable numbers, went this way? What were they looking for? Why did they come here?

The answer leads to the story, brief though it is, of Wystan, a Saxon saint of whom little is known save that he was the grandson of King Wiglaf, was murdered in 850 and buried in the mausoleum of his grandfather. A chronicler of these times goes on to say that 'miracles were not wanting at his martyrdom, for a column of light shot to Heaven from the place where he was murdered and remained visible for thirty days'.

This, then, was the beginning of what became a considerable cult, and the explanation of those worn steps. They were made by the feet of pilgrims come to visit the shrine of St Wystan, whose remains had been placed in this Saxon royal mausoleum, thus making of what is now the crypt of Repton Church a unique combination of royal burial-place with the shrine of a saint. Though little may be known of Wystan as a person, it is clear that his cult was not only powerful in its day, but continued a long time. There is evidence for this in the Chronicles of Evesham Abbey, one of the very great monastic centres of the Midlands and indeed of England. According to these Chronicles, King Cnut, who lived in the early part of the eleventh century, 'caused that glorious martyr to be moved from Repton to Evesham'. His miracles appear to have continued there, because the Chronicles give a list of them. They further state that a portion of his relics was returned to what was by that time a Norman priory at Repton in the thirteenth century.

But how did this place achieve its original importance as an ecclesiastical centre with royal connections in those far-off times when the Christian faith was brought to the Midlands by missionaries from the North? The trail here leads back to the soldier hermit St Guthlac, the very same man who landed from a boat in the Lincolnshire Fens to seek the solitary life where Crowland Abbey now stands. An account of his life records that he was trained by, or at any rate received his monastic tonsure from, the Abbess Aelfthryth at Repton. Therefore, before the year 700, there was in this place one of those double monasteries such as existed at Whitby and Coldingham and elsewhere, although probably on a smaller scale. But by the time King Ethelbald and King Wiglaf came to be buried it was already a place of religious and royal importance. The usual terrible fate overtook it with the coming of the Danes, a scourge so often encountered on this pilgrim journey already. According to the *Anglo-Saxon Chronicle* a Danish army spent the winter here in 874. This occuption certainly brought an end to the Saxon double monastery. Its successor was an Augustinian priory founded at Repton in 1172, remnants of which are now merged into some of the picturesque buildings of the school. The survivor of all these events, so tough and persistent can such a cult be, was St Wystan himself, to whose relics pilgrims were still resorting far into the Middle Ages.

This crypt at Repton continues to excite archaeologists: not all of its mysteries have yet been revealed, and there were extensive investigations continuing as late as 1976. But, to the traveller, the reward of coming here is the impression the place gives of the continuing power of the cult of a saint, however obscure. Those worn steps downwards into the chamber catch the eye; and it is possible, without too much imagination, to see still descending them the ghosts of those rough-and-ready pilgrims who came in such numbers and for so long to visit, either for healing or penance or simple wonderment, this chilly shrine, so oddly mixed up with the burial-place of kings.

Lichfield and the most holy Chad

When I last went to Lichfield I walked straight into an immense flower festival, and a very remarkable spectacle it was, every nook and corner in the immense cathedral occupied by some composition in flowers illustrative of a theme. The place was filled, too, not only with flowers but with people, so that a general air of life and enthusiasm was very evident. The contrast between this and that silent crypt at Repton, from which I had come was inescapable. In Repton there had been the past; here in Lichfield was a living present, as though in Lichfield were to be encountered, as is indeed the case, the still living tradition of a saint whose cult was one of the most popular in the Middle Ages – Chad.

He was the brother of St Cedd. Both of them had been pupils of Aidan at Lindisfarne, and the fact that here in the Midlands the name of Chad is still so much one to be reckoned with, shows how long was the reach and powerful the effect of that missionary enterprise which spread down from the North, carrying Christianity to the kingdoms of Saxon England. Chad himself began, and continued all his life, a missionary at heart. A simple and holy man, very much in the Celtic tradition, he loved to make his journeys humbly on foot, commending his message everywhere by the simple goodness of his character. According to Bede, so strong was Chad's preference for walking, that it required a direct order from the Archbishop of Canterbury, Theodore, to make him ride whenever he undertook a long journey. 'The Archbishop', says Bede, 'who recognised his outstanding holiness and considered it more proper for him to ride, himself insisted on helping him to mount his horse.'

This was when Chad had become Bishop of the Mercians and established his episcopal seat in what is now Lichfield. He came there straight from Lastingham where, in the crypt described earlier in this journey, what was very probably his altar still stands. He had succeeded his brother Cedd in the governance of that remote monastery and before that had been for a time, during a prolonged absence in Rome of Wilfrid of Ripon, Bishop of Northumbria. When, however, Wilfrid returned, and Archbishop Theodore, perhaps feeling that Chad's Celtic ordination was irregular, asked him to withdraw, he humbly and gladly did so. But clearly, the Archbishop had noted his qualities and, when opportunity offered, asked Oswey, King of the Mercians, to receive Chad as their bishop. He died some two and a half years later of the plague, foreseeing the coming of his end, and disclosing the matter to none other than Ovin who, having been Etheldreda's thane at Ely, had gone to Lastingham to work

The present Lichfield Cathedral is the third to stand on this site, with its three spires and ornate West Front it is an impressive sight. (*A. F. Kersting*)

as a lay brother in his old age, as was described in the earlier part of this journey, and now had been taken by Chad to Lichfield. It was this Ovin who used to tell the tale of how, about this time, when Chad was praying alone in his oratory, the sound of joyful singing was to be heard coming down from Heaven. Suddenly Chad threw open his window and called to Ovin to go to the church and fetch seven of the brethren back. To them he announced his imminent passing. When they had returned to the church, to pray about this sad tidings, Ovin stayed behind to ask Chad what had been the music which he had heard. To this Chad replied: 'They were angelic spirits, who came to summon me to the heavenly reward that I have always hoped and longed for, and they promised to return in seven days and take me with them.'

Chad died seven days later and, years afterwards, Bede heard of a man who at that time had seen a vision in which the soul of Chad's brother Cedd, descended from Heaven accompanied by angels, and carried him away to the heavenly kingdom. Such legends readily gathered about the name of Chad who, like Cuthbert, was a remarkable person; most loving, most winning, most holy. The greatest of his achievements during his short time in Mercia arose from these very qualities, for he was the first Bishop to draw together those long-estranged peoples, the Britons and the Angles.

He was not the first Bishop of Mercia, the Midland realm of Anglo-Saxon England. Indeed, his predecessor, one Diuma, had had his see at Repton. But Chad moved into Staffordshire and had his cell at a place called Stowe, some half a mile from the present Lichfield Cathedral. His body was shortly afterwards transferred to that site. Bede's account of what happened at both these places is as good a description as any of the kind of wonders which were associated then, and for centuries afterwards, with the shrine of a saint.

> Frequent miracles of healing attested to his virtues. . . . A madman wandering at large arrived there one evening, and passed the night in church unnoticed and unheeded by the watchman. And in the morning, to the amazement and delight of all, he left the place in his right mind, showing clearly what healing he had been granted there by the goodness of God. Chad's burial place is covered by a wooden tomb made in the form of a little house with an aperture in

the wall through which those who visit it out of devotion may insert their hand and take out some of the dust. They mix this in water and give it to sick men or beasts to drink, by which means their ailment is completely relieved and they are returned to the longed-for joys of health.

There was a well near Chad's oratory in which, it was said, he would, as a discipline of the flesh, stand in the cold water as he prayed. This well is in a garden next to St Chad's Church now, and it was once a Maundy Thursday custom to dress it with branches and flowers. It is interesting, in the light of this, that the custom of well-dressing survives in this region, certainly in Derbyshire, to this present time, which may well have been one of several pagan customs absorbed into Christianity as that faith spread. Early Christian missionaries frequently adopted this policy. Thus, as in St Augustine's Church in Canterbury there is a large black stone which clearly was once a pagan object of veneration, so, buried behind the high altar of the present Lichfield Cathedral, is another similar object which may well have once been the altar stone of a pagan temple. But holy wells, associated with saintly miracles in many places, have a very old tradition indeed, and maybe there is something in all of us which responds to this magic of water. I remember on several occasions taking parties of visitors to the Holy Land to see Jacob's Well on the road to Samaria, where the Orthodox priest in charge would always haul up a bucketful and allow members of the party to drink if they so wished. They almost invariably did. For that matter the pools of Bethesda and Siloam in Jerusalem, with their purported healing properties, were certainly in this tradition.

The present Lichfield Cathedral, largely built in the thirteenth and fourteenth centuries, is the third to stand on this site. To look upon the great building now is to realise how far it has developed from the 'little house' which Bede described as the resting-place of Chad's body. Even so, Lichfield Cathedral springs from Chad, was created to enshrine his body, and was through the ages a centre of his cult and the place of his shrine. With its three spires and astonishingly ornate West front, it is an impressive sight: but it has known its full share of the changes and chances of fortune since Bishop Roger de Clinton set about its first rebuilding. A later bishop, Walter de Langton, at his own cost created a rich shrine for Chad in a customary place behind the high altar, to which pilgrims came in very great numbers. Here, as elsewhere, the head of the Saint, separated from the body, was used as a secondary shrine and placed in the Chapel of the Head of St Chad, which is still there south of the choir. This head is no longer there. But, strangely enough, some other relics of the Saint are to be found to this day, not in Lichfield at all, but in St Chad's Roman Catholic Cathedral in Birmingham, to which some person or persons unknown must have presented them when that cathedral was created centuries later.

Worcester: St Oswald and St Wulstan

I suppose I must declare an interest here, as a canon of Worcester, who has lived a long time close by its tower within the sound of its bells. But it is not just partiality which leads me to say that this very beautiful and ancient foundation is one which needs to be known, and which rewards a pilgrim visit, more than some which attract the crowds today. It is true that many visitors come to Worcester; but scarcely in the numbers which go to such places as Norwich or Durham and many another, maybe because it lies just a little off the main lines of communication. But the small city is ancient and welcoming and the cathedral has a site overlooking the river scarcely less impressive than that of Durham. It has also, and was built around, two important saints: Oswald and Wulstan.

The best way to enter the cathedral, where their shrines were, is to take the way which mediaeval pilgrims followed, and to enter, not by the heavily restored North porch; but through the ancient Edgar Tower which is on the southern side. Immediately on the right is a Georgian house set in a handsome green. Where this house stands was once the Almonry at which pilgrims of the poorer sort could ask for free food and shelter. There is a charming effigy of one such pilgrim just below the vault at the west end of the South choir aisle.

On the right again across a lawn, are the ruins of what obviously was once a great building. This was the Guesten Hall, where pilgrims could be lodged and which was foolishly left to fall into disrepair by Victorian canons who did not know what to do with it. Beyond this again is an archway leading to the beautiful cloisters. At the end of the eastern arm of these cloisters is an ancient passageway through which the Prior and his guests

Effigy of King John on his tomb before the High Altar in Worcester Cathedral. The figures represent the saints Oswald and Wulstan whose shrines at one time stood on either side of the royal tomb. (*A. F. Kersting*)

could pass from his house into the cathedral. And there, before the high altar, is the tomb of King John. On either side of him is an effigy, one of St Oswald, and the other of St Wulstan. And hereby hangs a tale.

John, an evil king, was much attracted by Worcester's saints, whose cult, following the translation of their relics into the choir in the later years of his reign, was at the height of its popularity. In his will he requested that, in return for gifts to the monastery at Worcester, he should be buried between the two shrines, and that he should be so buried wearing the cowl of a monk in the expectation that, in such holy company and in such a guise, he would stand a better chance of entering Paradise. John died in 1216, the year after he had been compelled to sign Magna Carta, and his remains were brought to Worcester from Newark, where his death took place. He lies now alone, because the shrines have gone, but the names of Oswald and Wulstan are still of much importance to any who would explore the pilgrim trail through England.

In time, Oswald comes first. The son of a pagan Norseman settled in the English Danelaw, he was brought up as a Christian. His uncle, Odo, became Archbishop of Canterbury in 942, and it was he who, deeply influenced by the new, reformed monasticism then spreading all over France from the Abbey of Cluny, guided Oswald to become a monk with the special concern of establishing such reformed communities in England. Oswald succeeded the great Dunstan as Bishop of Worcester in 960, and four years later expelled the married clerks and began to convert the community to a full Benedictine monastery which it remained, until the Dissolution. It was Oswald who rebuilt the cathedral at Worcester and rededicated it to St Mary. Associated with St Dunstan and St Ethelwold for most of his public life it was natural that, when he died, by which time he was also Archbishop of York, popular veneration joined his name with theirs. He has been revered ever since as one of the three saints who revived English monasticism.

Inevitably, his remains were believed to possess miraculous powers. When pestilence was raging in the city, or an enemy was threatening to attack, the body of Oswald was carried through the streets and his help evoked to avert disaster. He was first buried on the south side of the altar of the church which he had built; but when this was pulled down a place for his shrine was needed in the new cathedral. So the eastern end of Wulstan's crypt was used for this purpose. It is necessary only to look hard at the stonework in the easternmost niche, beyond the altar in this beautiful place, to see that the lower level of stonework, differing from that which is above, was the place where the remains could have rested. Pilgrims went down to this crypt, and, as elsewhere, went round by the shrine, where they offered prayers and made their gifts, and then ascended to the body of the church by another staircase. A dramatic discovery, of an entirely new one was made during my time at Worcester. I saw it happen, and will not forget it. Excavation having been made down through the floor of the choir aisle on the south side, there was revealed a stone stairway, its steps still in perfect condition, bearing the traces of much traffic. On the walls was painted a pattern of flowers still undimmed after more than 1,000 years, and the archway which, being penetrated to reveal this new entry to the crypt, was in perfect order. It was after the canonisation of the other Worcester saint, Wulstan, that the remains of Oswald were moved up to the choir.

Wulstan was a very great man. Among his many distinctions is that he was the only Englishman allowed, after the Norman Conquest, to retain his see. There is a legend of what happened when, with other English bishops, he was required to attend a gathering in Westminster Abbey to hand over their crosiers to their Norman successors. When it came to his turn he duly laid down his upon the tomb of Edward the Confessor, and Lanfranc, the Norman Archbishop of Canterbury, commanded it to be taken up by the man appointed as Wulstan's successor. But he could not move it, nor could any of those who tried afterwards. In the end, Lanfranc commanded that Wulstan should keep it, and also his see of Worcester, whereupon the Bishop picked up his crosier again without difficulty.

He was born about 1008 and his father was probably a thane of the church of Worcester under St Oswald. He soon became Prior of the monastery and earned a reputation for sanctity through his care for the poor and through his preaching. He succeeded in suppressing the slave trade through Bristol to Ireland, which had been flourishing in his time, secured the building of many new parish churches, began the rebuilding of the cathedral at Worcester, where the crypt is a memorial to his zeal. In his day there was a close connection between the monks of Worcester and those of the see of Dublin, and the second Bishop there, Patrick, was a former monk of Worcester and wrote a splendid poem in Wulstan's honour. Wulstan died in 1095, and was canonised in 1203.

That event had been brought about by an odd sequence of events. Legend has it that towards the end of the twelfth century the dead Bishop requested through visions that his body should be moved. So one September night the Worcester monks approached Wulstan's tomb, opened it, and found the corpse still dressed in remnants of his clerical garments, the body not powder, but still skin and bone, which relics were placed in caskets upon the high altar. In 1201 began the miracles which were so long associated with them. A woman was cured after coming to pray for Wulstan's help: soon stories of cures spread far and wide. Fifteen were reported in one day. Eventually the Pope sent the Archbishop of Canterbury, the Bishop of Ely and

'St Wulstan, without difficulty, lifted his staff from the tomb.' (St Wulstan at Westminster with the Norman Bishops.)

the Abbots of Bury St Edmunds and Woburn to enquire into the truth of the stories. A document in Worcester Cathedral's library states: 'They, impressed with the glory and the multitude of proof, returned rejoicing.'

So Wulstan was canonised at Rome with great solemnity in 1203, one result of which was a great increase in the number of pilgrims visiting the shrine. Wulstan became for the Midlands what St Cuthbert was for the North and St Thomas at Canterbury for the South. This would have been when King John developed his interest in the shrine. Another King, Edward I, came eight

times to pray there and solicit the help of the Saint. Merchants came, farmers came, peasants came. Worcester became rich upon the proceeds. In 1218, with elaborate ceremony and in the presence of the young King Henry III, eleven bishops, seventeen abbots, and many of the nobility, a great service was held by the shrines of Oswald and Wulstan to mark the restoration of the cathedral after damage by fire. On this occasion Bishop Silvester ended an eloquent address in words which show what a great pilgrim cathedral could be in the Middle Ages. 'This, dear brethren, is also a place of safety, a port for the tempest tossed in which the anchorage is sure. Here by the prayer of priests, men accused of crime may find sure refuge. Venerate therefore the houses of God. Come to them with hearts free from all crime to make offerings of your souls.'

But strange were the customs of the age. Only part of Wulstan's body was placed in the shrine, for this same Bishop cut up the body and gave pieces of it to several of the abbots present: the Abbot of St Albans for one, as a special favour received a rib. When he returned, he placed in his monastery an altar to Wulstan, and over it a casket containing the relic.

Hereford, Ethelbert and St Thomas Cantilupe

Of the two saints particularly associated with Hereford, the first, Ethelbert, illustrates a very curious feature of the veneration accorded them in former times. It is that sudden death, especially death treacherously or unjustly met, irrespective of any merit or the lack of it in the person concerned, was almost a guarantee of a cult becoming attached to their memory and frequently to their remains. Nothing whatever, for instance, is known about the personal qualities of Ethelbert. What is known is that he was a king of the Angles, treacherously murdered during a visit to the palace of the King of Mercia, Offa, in Hereford, to which he had gone as a suitor to Offa's daughter. His death, which is said to have been instigated by Alfrida, Offa's wife, may have been due to some jealousy of him. The legend states that on the night of his burial a column of light rose towards the sky and that, three nights afterwards, the dead man appeared in a vision to a friend asking him to have his body removed to the monastery near Hereford. Miraculous events, it was said, began shortly afterwards at his tomb, so much so that, in the first half of the eleventh century a splendid shrine was made, and pilgrims came in numbers to it.

This shrine was destroyed in a Welsh raid in 1055, and when the cathedral was rebuilt, many years later, another was erected and continued to be popular right up until the Dissolution. But in

The Shrine of St Thomas Cantilupe in Hereford Cathedral. As at St Albans, and elsewhere, the relics of the saint would have stood on top of the shrine. (*Dean and Chapter of Hereford Cathedral*)

the interim the fortunes of Hereford in this respect flagged until the second saint of this place came upon the scene.

This was Thomas de Cantilupe, Bishop of Hereford 1275–82, who, on a journey to Rome, died of the plague. His chaplain, being required to bring home the body, boiled it, as was the custom, returning with bones which were then deposited in the Lady chapel at Hereford. Miracles soon began: the shrine became one of the most popular in the West Midlands. Three hundred cures were claimed to have been effected at the tomb to which, on one occasion, Edward I sent a wax model of his favourite falcon, which was sick, thus revealing an interesting practice common to all shrines for which healing properties were claimed: a quantity of wax would be sent, either in the form of a taper corresponding to the length of the giver, or in mass equal to his weight. There would be nothing unusual in the King sending a model in wax of his falcon, since aid could be sought and often was, for animals and birds as well as for humans. What remains, and it is considerable, of the shrine of Thomas Cantilupe at Hereford is in itself interesting. The lower part, in the shape of a tomb, bears carvings of figures of Knights Templars, of which order, originally founded to guard pilgrims' routes to the Holy Land, Thomas was Provincial Grand Master. Above is a marble base

where the reliquary box, tent-shaped, once stood housing those bones. His flesh and entrails were buried in the monastery of San Severo, near Orvieto, his heart at Ashridge.

This is by no means the whole of the story. Not only was Cantilupe the last Englishman canonised in the fourteenth century and one of the last saints created before the Dissolution. He also came to have attached to his name the largest collection of healing miracles, second only to those of Thomas Becket of Canterbury, to have survived on record. The process of canonisation of Cantilupe was detailed and prolonged. Richard Swinfield, the Chaplain who had been with him when he died, and who succeeded him as Bishop of Hereford, took his cause to the highest level, writing to the Pope and eventually gaining the support of the monarch himself, Edward I. Commissioners of enquiry were appointed; proceedings were undertaken both in London and in Hereford; witnesses were called, long lists of miracles were compiled. Before all this was concluded, Edward I had been succeeded by his son, Edward II, who also lent his support to the matter. Eventually, by 1320, Thomas Cantilupe, Bishop of Hereford, was a canonised saint. But, long before this, he had been the centre of a popular cult, and a witness to the enquiry in 1307 stated that 'even from two hundred leagues away people came on pilgrimage to the Hereford church and hastened to his tomb as if to a saint'. When the preliminary enquiries leading to his canonisation were in progress, evidence was produced to show how his burial-place was already festooned with gifts of the faithful, wax animals, crutches, offerings of gold and precious cloth, rings and jewels of all sorts. It is clear that the miracles attributed to his powers increased in number as his cause was pressed and his praises sung. Rumour fed upon rumour, and the more the tale of Cantilupe was spread around, the more pilgrims hastened to his shrine.

It is odd that Cantilupe of Hereford has been so forgotten as the centuries have passed. All that remains now is this shrine, with the figures of Knights Templars carved upon it. There is, however, one more visible and notable memorial: the central tower of Hereford Cathedral, largely paid for by the offerings of pilgrims.

For me, Hereford has been familiar ground for a long time: the friendly cathedral, with its many other treasures, being always a joy to visit. But not far away, on a westward slope of the Cotswolds, just outside the little town of Winchcombe, lies a rare spot – Hailes Abbey, with its extraordinary tale of the Holy Blood. Here is encapsulated an almost perfect example of the rise and fall of the cult of a relic, from beginning to end in every detail, typical of so much that happened in Pilgrim's England in days gone by.

The Holy Blood of Hailes

One day in the October of 1242, a nobleman Richard, Earl of Cornwall, who also used of himself the questionable title of King of the Romans, found himself in peril of his life in a storm at sea as he was returning to England. In this extremity he made a vow that, should his life be spared, he would found a monastery dedicated to the glory of God. His brother, Henry III, three years later gave him the manor of Hailes in order that he could fulfil his vow. Thus it came about that, as a daughter house of the Cistercian Abbey of Beaulieu in Hampshire, Hailes was founded as a monastic community and was dedicated, in the presence of the King and Queen and Earl Richard himself, in the November of 1251. It was to be one of the last Cistercian houses to be founded in England.

But it was not until 1270 that that event took place which was to bring fame to this obscure and isolated community. Earl Richard had a second son, who presented to Hailes a phial of the Holy Blood, said to be the authentic blood of Christ himself. Indeed, it was more than purported. When Edmund bought this object from the Count of Flanders it bore the guarantee of the Patriarch of Jerusalem, later to be Pope Urban IV. One is reminded of how, centuries before this, when Wilfrid of Ripon bought his collection of relics in Rome, genuineness was guaranteed by the 'elect men', or reputable agents, from whom he had them. The Blood of Hailes, in its little phial, bearing so distinguished a guarantee as that of the Patriarch himself, was clearly an object of great note, and it was the possession of this which made of Hailes Abbey a great pilgrimage centre. Now thanks to excellent excavations and clearance carried out by the Department of the Environment, the actual place where it stood in its shrine can be seen among the green grass of the ruins, behind the high altar. Around it, and especially built for the purpose, were chapels and a processional way for pilgrims. Thereafter, right up until the time of the Dissolution and through periods of varying fortunes for the

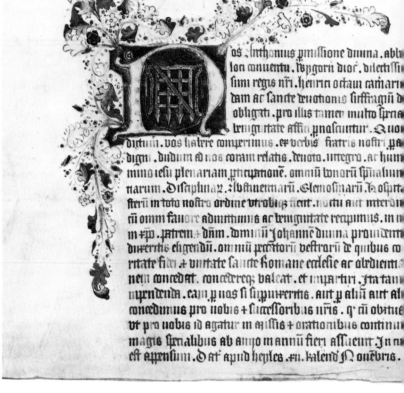

A certificate of indulgence as issued at Hailes Abbey, Gloucestershire, in 1509.
Such documents, promising remission of sin by virtue of pilgrimage being made
to a sacred shrine, were eagerly sought after by pilgrims. The sale of them was an
important part of the income of some shrines. (*Department of the Environment*)

abbey itself, they continued to come. Hugh Latimer, subsequently Bishop of Worcester, and a martyr burnt at the stake
under Mary Tudor, was in 1533 Vicar of Kineton near Warwick,
near by a very ancient roadway. He wrote: 'I live within half a
mile of the Fosseway and you would wonder to see how they
come by flocks out of the West Country to many images; but
chiefly to the Blood of Hailes.'

It is fascinating to think about these pilgrims, and there can be
no better place to do so than in the middle of the remains of Hailes
Abbey, now at last cleared from the overgrowth of time. On a

maria

[Latin manuscript text in gothic script]

heples

summer day, such as the one when I was there, the trees rustle, the sheep – the abbey once made a considerable part of its income from the wool of their predecessors – move quietly upon the hills around. It must have been summer when the great majority of pilgrims came, for it would have been impossible for them to move through the muddy tracks of winter, whether on foot or horseback. When they arrived at Hailes they would have seen, impressively, the great church, the stumps of the pillars of which can be seen now. At the eastern end would be the shrine of the Holy Blood, before which they would pass, awed by its suspended lights and, maybe, by monkish voices singing the offices in the great choir. There would be glimpses of the cloister and of the monastic buildings around. And, when night fell, there would be shelter for them at the pilgrim's hostel the site of which is marked on the map of the area to be seen in the Abbey Museum recently created at Hailes.

The Holy Blood, dimly to be perceived in its vessel, would be revealed by its attendants at intervals. Pilgrims would pray before it, and, in the immemorial way, ask for forgiveness or for healing or, in simple wonderment, give thanks for this miraculous sight.

In 1538, no more than five years after Latimer's comment, orders were issued to the commissioners of Thomas Cromwell for the suppression of all shrines. In the October of that same year they visited Hailes and removed the Holy Blood to London where it was displayed by the Bishop of Rochester preaching at St Paul's Cross. On that occasion he declared that the Blood, certified so long ago by the Patriarch of Jerusalem, was in fact 'honey clarified and coloured with saffron, as has been evidently proved before the King and his Council'.

Fifteenth-century seal of Hailes Abbey. The central figure is probably Richard, Earl of Cornwall. The bottle with a cross in the mouth in the right hand symbolises the Holy Blood. The left hand holds a sprinkler. (*The British Library*)

The last Abbot pensioned off settled down near by. There is a letter from him to the Crown now to be seen in the Abbey Museum. He received £100 a year. The abbey buildings were sold to a certain Richard Andrews, a dealer in monastic property, and soon afterwards demolished. So silence fell, and prevailed for many years, over the site of Hailes Abbey until, in the seventeenth century, a manor house was formed out of what had been the Abbot's lodging. This in turn vanished away and it is only very recently that the site of the place which once housed the miraculous Blood of Hailes has been won back from the surrounding grass and woodland. So there it is, a perfect example, from beginning to end, of the rise and fall of the cult of a relic. As to the Blood, the Bishop of Rochester, at the end of his sermon at Paul's Cross, poured it upon a fire.

A royal saint at Gloucester

From Hailes, through Winchcombe and over Clee Hill it is an easy and short journey to Gloucester. But the cathedral, massive and very Norman, rather like Durham, seems a world away from the gentler beauties of Hereford and Worcester and Lichfield. Embedded among its splendours, in the great choir, dominated by its marvellous Crécy window, is the tomb of one of the most improbable saints to be found in England, Edward II. This tomb is in itself a remarkable creation. The figure, the work of a master craftsman from the Court of Edward III, is in alabaster and dates from about 1340: the face, although probably not a portrait, is striking. There are angels at the head, a lion at the feet: stags carved upon the tomb are said to represent the animals which drew the bier at the royal funeral. This King is an uncanonised saint; representations made to Rome for his canonisation in the time of Edward III all failed. The fact remains that his tomb received great veneration, and drew many pilgrims. The wonderful choir at Gloucester was to a considerable extent paid for out of their offerings.

Yet the whole thing seems inexplicable. It is certainly a reminder that there was, in earlier times, not felt to be any necessary connection between the virtues of a person and his subsequent canonisation. It is easy for us to think of a Cuthbert or a St Thomas of Canterbury as a saint because they were clearly

men of spiritual qualities, but former ages did not think in this manner. A saint, whether subsequently canonised or not, could attract popular favour by the manner of his death, by the circumstances of his birth especially if he were of royal blood – and sometimes by the vigour with which his cause could be promoted by those who, as was certainly the case with the monks at Gloucester, felt themselves in need of a saint.

All these features can be found in the case of Edward II at Gloucester, who, not in any sense an admirable character, was weak, was as a king disastrous and had a propensity for cultivating favourites such as Piers Gaveston, causing great offence to his people. They did not protest when he was deposed from the throne: what aroused popular fervour was the manner of his death. When Edward escaped into Wales he was recaptured by the forces of the frightful Queen Isabella, the 'She-wolf of France', in 1327 and was taken to Berkeley Castle, near Gloucester. There, his original noble custodian, Lord Berkeley having been removed, he was put to death in the most horrible manner, it was said that his shrieks of despair were heard by the villagers and that he ended his life 'with a lamentable loud cry heard by many of the town and the castle'. Abbot Thokey of Gloucester asked that he should have the body for burial, others probably having not cared to risk the vengeance of the Queen by taking it themselves. So Edward was taken to the monastery at Gloucester and buried within the church.

With the coming of Edward III, following the downfall of Queen Isabella, the new King raised the stately tomb which now stands in the choir at Gloucester, to honour the remains. It was almost certainly a political act, just as Edward II is an example of a political saint. In the eyes of the new monarch anything which underlined the enormities of the previous regime was to be encouraged.

Miracles were said to have taken place at the tomb straight away, and rumours of them spread. Pilgrims came, greatly increasing the wealth of the monastery which, hitherto, had lacked a saint as a source of income. But this cult of a murdered sovereign remains difficult to explain, seeming, as one later writer, Dean Spence, put it:

Alabaster head of Edward II on his tomb in the quire in Gloucester Cathedral. The work is that of a master craftsman and dates from about 1340. (*A. F. Kersting*)

As though men in England felt that a curse lay on them, and on their homes and hearths, owing to their having suffered the Lord's anointed to be cruelly done to death in their midst. So thousands came and prayed at the dead King's shrine. Their offerings enriched the Abbey coffers. Soon there was wealth enough to have rebuilt the whole church from its very foundations. At all events, the desire of the monks to adorn their ancient house with new work could now be gratified.

There are three elements in the creation of a cult which can be clarified from this case of Edward II. The first is the veneration often accorded to the victims of violent death, the explanation of which is probably to be found in the fact that, in the early Church, martyrs were venerated and, since they themselves frequently came to violent ends in times of persecution, the connection between such deaths and the holiness of those who suffered them was established. The case of Ethelbert, that King of the East Angles who was murdered on a visit to Hereford, comes immediately to mind.

Another element is the immemorial fascination of, and veneration for, royal blood. To slay a king was to lay hands on the Lord's anointed, an act of sacrilege, among crimes something special. How strongly this feeling has persisted through the ages can be seen by the reactions to the execution of Charles I, when people below the scaffold dipped handkerchiefs in his blood and when the whole country lamented what was felt to be a fearful act. The execution of King Louis in the French Revolution more than a century later caused a similar reaction. Finally, there was the matter of opportunism. The monks of Gloucester, as has been noted, needed a saint. By an amalgam of all these elements, and by the historic chance of the singularly violent death of Edward II they got one.

In the middle of Gloucester is the New Inn, said to have been created originally for the reception of pilgrims to the tomb of Edward. That may well have been the case. If so, this is one of the few pilgrim inns, in the full sense, to be found. As a general rule, and certainly in the earlier days, pilgrims would be received at the monastery which held the shrine, and there housed in a 'guesten hall', as at, for example, Worcester. They would also be received in a religious manner by the kiss of peace, which is the origin of the term 'salutation' still to be found in the name of some inns. It was always the case that inns, or lodging-places, would be needed between the actual shrines, especially if the journey to them was long. But the New Inn at Gloucester, with its charming gallery over a central courtyard, deserves a visit from the pilgrim now.

A king and a saint at Malmesbury

A king of a very different kind and quality from Edward II lies somewhere in or around Malmesbury Abbey. He certainly does not lie in his tomb which, though dignified and striking, is a mediaeval creation. But Athelstan was one of the greatest monarchs in Saxon history and indeed in England's history. Born in 895, he was the favourite grandson of Alfred, was the first monarch to be crowned on the King's Stone in the Market Place at Kingston upon Thames. He was a great warrior who magnificently carried on, and triumphed in, the long struggle which Alfred had begun against the Danish invaders. Athelstan conquered Northumbria, harried the Scots and overran Scotland as far as Aberdeen. He had a fleet which attacked the Orkneys. He beat a combined army of Scots and Welsh at the great Battle of Brunaburh. Glastonbury men greatly helped him in this conflict, and something of the extraordinary antiquity of the place is reflected in the fact that to this day descendants of the men who fought with him still receive by inheritance their due share of land known as the King's Heath which Athelstan gave to their predecessors in gratitude. He was a great collector of books, a friend of scholarship and in every way an admirable monarch.

He also had four beautiful sisters, all of whom made distinguished marriages. A by-product was that among their dowries were many relics such as pieces of the true Cross, the spear that pierced the side of our Saviour, a portion of the Crown of Thorns and so forth, many of which were given to Athelstan's favourite abbey – Malmesbury. It therefore happened that here at one time would have been one of the finest collections of relics on show anywhere in Europe, and this must have been among the many attractions which brought pilgrims.

But there was another, and a far greater attraction. Malmesbury was the home of St Aldhelm, 640–709. A Saxon by birth he was closely related to the kings of Wessex, and was a man of much influence and learning, singularly cultivated for his time,

Porch carvings of the Apostles, Malmesbury Abbey. The style and vigour of the work indicates a high level of Saxon art and civilisation. (*Rev. J. C. P. Barton, Malmesbury Vicarage*)

with a knowledge of Greek, and Latin and music. It was he who really founded Malmesbury Abbey, a noble place to this day, although what stands there now is but a fragment of the magnificence which it once had. To go there now is to feel the strength and the charm of the high noon of Saxon civilisation, brilliantly and beautifully evoked in the glorious porch with its wonderful carvings of the Apostles.

There is a statue in the Chapel of St Aldhelm showing the Saint holding a lyre, illustrative of a particularly endearing feature of the man, who put his knowledge of music, most unusually in his day, to popular use. Accompanying himself on the lyre, he would stand among crowds down in the town and sing and talk in open-air meetings reminiscent of Salvation Army gatherings in this present time. Then he would lead them back into the abbey for service. It was to his shrine that pilgrims particularly came after his death, and for long afterwards. They still go to Malmesbury, as I did myself, marvelling at, among much else, the quaint watching-loft, high up above the nave, from which a vigilant eye could be kept upon the many precious relics which once were in the place.

CHAPTER 6

The South: From Glastonbury to Winchester

Glastonbury – many mysteries and many saints
Shaftesbury – Edward the Martyr
Whitchurch Canonicorum – the shrine in a country church
Salisbury – St Osmund
Winchester – St Swithun

Glastonbury: Joseph of Arimathea, King Arthur and the Holy Grail

I have to confess that my first visit to Glastonbury was a failure. On that day in late August a steady drizzle blanketed everything; the 400-foot Glastonbury Tor with the solitary church tower on top of it was just able to emerge through low-lying cloud: the town was full of visitors giving every impression of not knowing where to go or what to look for and the main street was congealed with traffic. It was necessary, as far as I was concerned, to go away and return clearer in mind as to what this amazing place really signified, which is much, and able to view over-all in better conditions the very unusual landscape in which it stands and which is an essential component of its strangeness.

Glastonbury is unique in many ways: any place which can lay claim to have been, at one end of the spectrum of time, the abode of Joseph of Arimathea and possibly to have been visited by Christ himself and, in this present century, able to attract some people who believe it to be, in solar and terrestrial terms, one of the world's power points, may fairly claim that title. Glastonbury is also a very difficult place to understand: its story is immensely complex, and it is not a matter here of seeking out a saint and his shrine but of discovering why this Somersetshire town should

once have been the resting-place of many, including not only St Joseph of Arimathea himself, but also, according to some legends, of St Patrick and, this a belief on firmer foundations – of St Aidan of Lindisfarne, Paulinus of York and many another. And to this mix has to be added the whole body of Arthurian legend. Why is the reputed grave of King Arthur in this place? Is the near-by Isle of Avalon the mystery-shrouded place where he died, and was the Holy Grail, the cup used by Christ himself at the Last Supper, really brought here and buried under Chalice Hill. Clearly, this is not a mystery which can be resolved, even if it ever can be, by arriving on a rainy day full of traffic and expecting all to be made plain. For that reason I found it best, and only then after considerable study, to go to a high place near by and to look upon the surrounding scene until, bit by bit, its various elements began to merge together into the great canvas which is Glastonbury.

First, then, the landscape. Glastonbury Tor is a conical hill which rises out of what were the Somerset flatlands with the Mendip Hills on the one hand and the Quantock Hills on the other. At the top of the Tor is the tower of St Michael, where once stood a church of that dedication which fell down in the thirteenth century. Westward of this there is the smaller hill named Chalice, where, according to some of the many legends associated with the area, the vessel used at the Last Supper was buried and out of which now flows an inexhaustible spring. Southward are small beehive shaped hills. Below is the town: in the middle of it are the ruins of the abbey. Where the vale stretches away towards the Bristol Channel, a rise, in what was once an area entirely covered by marshland, is the Isle of Avalon. In the vale were once lake villages, the site of them still marked by mounds, and all of it is now rich in farms and orchards. Such is the Glastonbury setting.

Next, the Glastonbury story. This has two distinct elements: the legend of Joseph of Arimathea and, of an entirely different nature, of King Arthur and his knights and Avalon. These two elements merge in the legend of the Grail and in the reputed finding, in 1191, of the coffins of Arthur and his queen, Guinevere, whose burial-place is still there, in the midst of the abbey ruins, and is visited by tens of thousands annually.

Glastonbury Tor. Richard Whyting, the last Abbot of Glastonbury, was executed in front of the tower. (*A. F. Kersting*)

The legend of St Joseph of Arimathea, upon which the fame of Glastonbury mainly rested, and still does, begins with the belief that it was he, the same 'good and just man', as he is described in St Luke's Gospel, who after the Crucifixion requested from Pilate the body of Christ and gave it burial personally brought the faith to England, having been inspired to do so by the Apostle Philip who had himself acted as a missionary in Gaul. With him Joseph brought the Holy Grail which had been given to him by Pilate. In this cup Joseph had caught some of Christ's blood as it fell from the Cross and also some of his sweat which is why, in some representations of Joseph, such as that on the rood screen of Plymtree Church in Devon, he is shown holding two cruets. From the coast Joseph and his party made their way to Glastonbury where, upon a hill just south-west of the town, and now known as Wearyall Hill, he thrust his staff into the ground. This is the staff which is said to have instantly bloomed with white flowers and is the origin of what is still known as the Holy Thorn, very much in evidence at Glastonbury now and which does indeed flower at Christmas, when a spray of it is customarily sent to the Queen.

So Joseph settled in Glastonbury and there under angelic inspiration, built, so it was said, the first Christian church in this land. In one form of this story Jesus is said to have manifested himself in a vision and dedicated it in honour of his mother. In another, and later version of the legend, Joseph, a rich merchant trading in Cornish tin, brought with him the young Jesus as his nephew and that it was he who, during those years of his life, between boyhood and later manhood, of which nothing is said in the Gospels, himself, working as a carpenter, built the church in Glastonbury. It is possible to find here a key to something of the quite unusual importance which Glastonbury has always exercised upon the national imagination. It is a place which can be associated, through its legends, with the person of Christ himself and, since that cannot be claimed for any other country, it can be used as an element in giving to the English national identity a special importance in the divine scheme of things.

Nobody knows where Joseph of Arimathea was buried, although in later centuries unverified claims were made that the place had been discovered. But there is certainly no trace of, or claim for, this in the legend now. Before he died he is said to have buried the grail; but no one knows where. And this is the point at which the second element in the Glastonbury story, the

Arthurian, comes into the picture.

Clearly, this is not the place to elaborate upon the immensely complex development of the Arthur story – in itself far more involved and extensive than the history of Glastonbury. Let it therefore be sufficient at this point to say that the Arthurian material, based upon some historical fact and a great deal of later mediaeval legend with its roots in much earlier folklore, touches upon Glastonbury at two points; the identification of the Isle of Avalon as the place where Arthur died, and with the story of the quest for the Grail as developed, for instance, in the poem of Chretien de Troyes *Perceval* and to be found later in *Le Morte d'Arthur* of Malory in the fifteenth century. This goes right through to Tennyson in the nineteenth where Avalon is the place of Arthur's death. The same theme caught the imagination of the pre-Raphaelites, so that we have the famous painting by Burne-Jones of Arthur on his death-bed on the Isle of Avalon, a mysterious, tree-shaded abode of shadowy figures attending upon the departing. How, then, did Avalon come to be associated with Arthur's death? Some idea of the antiquity of the legend is reflected in a story contained in the biography of the sixth-century historian Gildas, wherein it is told that Guinevere was captured by the King of 'The Summer Region', in which phrase it is possible to discern the word Somerset. It was he who carried her off to 'Glastonia', a place surrounded by marshes. So the narrative line begins to close in on the link between Avalon and Arthur. One of the main sources is *The History of the Kings of England* by Geoffrey of Monmouth who, writing in 1135 and drawing, as he himself states, upon Welsh bardic legend, refers to an Isle of Avalon. He does not relate it to Glastonbury; but in a later work, the *Life of Merlin* he tells how Taliesin the bard sang of Arthur, dying, being taken to the 'Isle of Apples'. In a later variation of the tale, this kingdom of Melwas, which was the name of the King who carried off Guinevere, is described as an abode of the dead, 'a bourn from which no traveller returns'. True, Guinevere is rescued by Lancelot; but when Arthur's time comes, he vanishes into Avalon, perhaps to sleep, maybe even sometime, at a time of crisis for his people, to return, a fitting close to the legend of a hero so great that he could not be allowed to die. This legend was, as will be seen, a potent political force in

(*Overpage*) Glastonbury Abbey ruins. The alleged grave of King Arthur is in the centre of the nave just in front of the broken arch. (*A. F. Kersting*)

the time of Henry II and his dealings with the Welsh. Guinevere in the land of the dead, it might be added, and subsequently delivered, bears considerable resemblance to the Greek legend of Persephone, carried off by Pluto, King of the Underworld, and permitted to return only for half the year, bringing summer with her. Thus do legends bafflingly interweave in the Glastonbury picture. The story of the quest by Arthur and his companions for that Holy Grail which Joseph of Arimathea concealed at his death, bring the two main elements in the body of tradition together.

But if there is legend, there is also fact to stiffen it. Glastonbury has a real, as well as a mythical past, and its story holds historical figures, some of note, such as St Dunstan, Abbot in 940 and later Archbishop of Canterbury. Here is a very great man indeed. Born in the Glastonbury area not long after the death of Alfred, he became a protégé of King Athelstan whose tomb was discovered on this journey in Malmesbury Abbey. Athelstan has his court near Glastonbury and Dunstan was one of its luminaries. He became a monk: he was always a teacher: he was great enough to arouse the jealousies of lesser men – jealousies which were at one time a threat to his life – and holy enough to inspire a whole body of legend. This is the man who is said to have had a vision of the future great abbey which would be at Glastonbury; he who was said to have seized Satan by the nose; and it was Dunstan to whom King Edmund, the successor to Athelstan, when on the verge of a fatal accident while hunting in Cheddar Gorge, vowed that he would reinstate him in the position from which he had been banished if only his own life was spared. So Dunstan became Abbot of Glastonbury, inheriting what was virtually a ruin and beginning two major works of reconstruction; the first of the building itself, the second of the Benedictine rule by which it lived. Later, as Archbishop of Canterbury he became the close counsellor of King Edgar and, when that King died, took his body for burial at Glastonbury. He also died there and was soon recognised as a saint, with miracles following at his tomb. There followed an unedifying dispute between the monks of Canterbury and those of Glastonbury as to the whereabouts of his actual bones, Glastonbury claiming them but Canterbury stating that they had them. The latter claim eventually prevailed. Even so, Dunstan became and remained a very notable saint of Glastonbury.

Another figure in the history of the place, although of an

entirely different order, was the historian William of Malmesbury who visited the abbey in 1125 and, in the course of a long stay, completed a history which has remained of importance, even though much of it must be regarded as embroidered by imagination, as was the accepted custom of the time. The monks obviously told their important visitor many surprising things for him to record, such as that there was a church there in the year 166, even possibly earlier, according to some, built by missionaries from Rome and dedicated to the Blessed Virgin. They also showed him a charter dating from 601, setting forth the grant to the old church of land by a Celtic king.

William of Malmesbury certainly saw pilgrims in plenty at Glastonbury, which was even then a centre for pilgrims, the burial-place of many saints, one of them St Patrick who, retiring there after his work in Ireland, according to the story, attracted other Irish saints such as St Bridget. St David of Wales came there later, with seven bishops, wishing to consecrate the church but, being told in a dream that Christ had already done so, he consecrated a church which he built himself. Already, then, by the date of William of Malmesbury's visit, there was a great treasury of relics at Glastonbury, and there is considerable support also for the claim, upon which William of Malmesbury based much of his evaluation of the importance of Glastonbury, for the belief that relics of such saints as Aidan, Benedict Biscop and Paulinus of York, were brought down from the North at the time of the Danish raids, to keep them in security.

The historical shape of events in Glastonbury, as opposed to the legendary, from the earliest known times until the great fire of 1184 is, therefore, that when the Saxon King Ine of Wessex came to the region towards the end of the seventh century he found, huddled below the Tor, a Celtic monastery, most likely a collection of beehive huts, established and continued by Welsh or Irish monks, the whole centred upon that ancient church of wattle and daub which had even then for long been thought of as that which Joseph himself had created. No written account of this belief existed: all the Glastonbury records, for that matter, date from centuries later than the events which they purport to describe. The fact remains that the reputation of the area for sanctity was strong enough, when the Saxon Ine of Wessex arrived, to cause him to refound the monastery, refurbishing and enriching it by gifts.

The fire of 1184 was a huge disaster, destroying the ancient church, the tombs of kings, the relics of many saints. Yet out of it, phoenix-like, arose an even greater Glastonbury. Its connection was Joseph of Arimathea, so long a matter of folk memory, became, as written accounts began to appear, more clearly defined, and the association with Arthur was immensely reinforced by a very peculiar happening, to this day the subject of debate, which took place two years or so after the fire. This was the discovery, or so it was purported to be, by the monks, of the bodies of Arthur and Guinevere lying in a hollowed trunk of oak deep down within the abbey precincts. Also discovered was a cross bearing the inscription in Latin to the effect that 'here lies interred the body of King Arthur with Guinevere his wife, in the Isle of Avalon'.

Two things need to be said here: the first is that this might have been a politically inspired fake. Henry II, who encouraged the search for the grave – a monk of Glastonbury having claimed to have seen the place of it in a dream – was embroiled with an unquiet Wales at this time, where the belief that the heroic King, Arthur of memory, might one day awake from his sleep in Avalon and return to lead them to victory kept the disquiet alive. To prove him dead would therefore help to defuse this situation, so that the Glastonbury discovery was timely indeed. Secondly, it bears remembering that the first to record this happening was the Welsh historian, Geraldus Cambrensis, a colourful chronicler renowned more for imagination than accuracy. It was he who, in the account, for the first time bound together in the same golden cord of legend, Arthur, Avalon and Glastonbury. It needed only to add the notion, which was indeed added in later years, that Arthur himself was descended from Joseph of Arimathea, to give a final touch to a body of Glastonbury legend complex, extraordinary and persistent, and yet so difficult to grasp that it crumbles in the hand as the golden hair of Guinevere is said by Geraldus to have done when one of the monkish openers of the grave touched it. But this legend persisted: the historian Leland, two and a half centuries later, wrote that he actually saw, and indeed held in his hand, the cross which was found in the grave. And some modern specialists in Arthurian history have suggested that there might be more in this whole matter than that it was only a politically inspired imposture.

So on my further visit, with all this amazing story in mind, I found the abbey ruins with Arthur's grave amid them remarkably evocative; the Abbot's kitchen, St Joseph's chapel, where many relics once reposed, and Chalice Hill with its spring not only deeply interesting but also strangely disturbing. It was also impossible not to marvel at the rich overlay of contemporary eccentricity which has become attached to the place, such as that the signs of the zodiac can be plotted, given an aerial view, in the outlines of the surrounding countryside. And, among groups who have somehow heard Glastonbury calling to them there are the Essenes, who consider the place to be a cosmic power point and who believe that the Second Coming will take place there. Yet others claim that it is a very important point on a leyline, or prehistoric direction indicator, running between Glastonbury, through Stonehenge and beyond.

All in all, Glastonbury is a strange and haunted place; very difficult to account for, even more difficult to forget.

The shrine in a country church

From all these complexities and mysteries of Glastonbury it was a complete change to seek out the little shrine in the village church at Whitchurch Canonicorum a few miles north of Bridport. I went straight south from Glastonbury through Crewkerne to find this place, which involved a long and interesting cross-country route, for the most part through very quiet country until the minor road I was on dipped down into this village at the foot of a long hill. And there, in the centre of the place, was the ancient church, and within this church, beneath the north window of the north transept, was a shrine, similar in all respects to others to be found in many other places, which once contained the relics of a saint. The difference here is that this one still does. Therefore the shrine at Whitchurch Canonicorum is unique: the only one in a parish church in England still to contain the remains of the saint in whose name it was originally created. Here, in this Dorset village church, in this tomb still known locally as the 'Saint's shrine' are relics which not only were once venerated but which still seem to attract modern pilgrims in a peculiar way, as we shall see. There was a time when many pilgrims' paths led to this place and, judging by the number of cars parked outside, there is still a steady summer stream of their successors.

At the very beginning of this book I said that, in the matter of pilgrimage, we are 'in the presence of a living tradition. The fact that so many of the relics of mediaeval pilgrimage are ruins, does not mean that they do not still have power in them. It is as though, moving round a partially demolished house, we were to touch wires left dangling from a wall and receive a shock, because they are still mysteriously alive.' The truth of those words is dramatically illustrated in this church at Whitchurch Canonicorum. It is a strange thing to see, on entering, the votive crosses cut in the stonework of the porch by pilgrims of long ago. But it is even stranger to see the coins thrown in by pilgrim visitors now through the oval apertures in the shrine, and to observe the notes written on scraps of paper likewise placed within. One of them which I picked up on the day of my visit read: 'Asking for help at my operation, and for strength for all my family.' Just to read that note was ample reward for the long cross-country journey south; just to see those coins was to experience the electric shock coming from recognition of this still living tradition, if only dimly comprehended, of an ancient pilgrim cult.

So whose is this shrine, with its lower portion of early-thirteenth-century work supporting an upper portion with a Purbeck marble top? The oval openings beneath, where people now put their coins and their curious notes, were once used, in the customary manner, by those seeking healing who put in them their diseased limbs, hoping for healing, or pieces of cloth or other objects which they could then take away back home to help in somebody else's healing, as they believed. The name of the saint whose remains are within is St Candida, or St Wite. This is known for certain, because in 1900 when a crack appeared in the North wall of the transept, the shrine was damaged and, in the necessary repairs which followed, the tomb was opened. Inside was found a leaden box. On the box was an inscription in Latin which read 'here rest the remains of St Wite', and in the box were a number of bones thought to be those of a woman. The question therefore is, who was she?

For many centuries it was believed that St Wite was a Saxon woman killed by the Danes on one of their raids on the nearby coast when they slew those whom they did not enslave. The fact that she was in due course venerated as a saint suggests that she was a Christian, and the rise of her cult might be attributed to that 'violent death syndrome' so often found in that context. However, in later times other guesses have been made as to the identity of this mysterious saint in the shrine at Whitchurch

'The oval openings were used . . . by those seeking healing who put in them their diseased limbs.' (The shrine at Whitchurch Canonicorum.)

Canonicorum. The Victorian writer, Baring-Gould, for instance, in his *Lives of the Saints* suggested that she could have been a Celtic princess who, having married a prince of Brittany, took the French name of Blanche, which in Latin would be, more or less, Candida. He further suggests that, later in her life, she was captured by pirates, escaped and walked on the water back to Brittany, where the foam of the turning tide is sometimes still called the track of St Blanche. But this is highly fanciful. When I was writing the biography of Baring-Gould I discovered what a highly imaginative writer he was, especially when concerned with the stories of Celtic saints. Another theory has been that Wite was a Wessex-born monk who, when travelling with a band of missionaries under St Boniface in Germany, was massacred and his body brought back for burial. The difficulty here is obviously that the bones in this little casket at Whitchurch Canonicorum were the bones of a woman.

But what does it matter? That the old tradition that St Wite was a Saxon woman killed by the Danes is still locally accepted was shown by the design which I saw on a kneeler in the church, which clearly showed a woman on the shore with a Viking ship threateningly approaching. But for those visitors who, acting almost unconsciously as pilgrims at a shrine, had put their money through the apertures into the tomb, or for that man who had asked for help at his forthcoming operation, it would be a matter of no concern whatever. What did matter apparently, was the sense of some power coming from it which could be of help.

Shaftesbury by way of Sherborne

'Speak only praise of Sherborne', wrote S. H. Burton, a noted authority on West Country life. It is indeed a lovely little town and I am glad I went there because in this place, clustered around its beautiful abbey, is so much of the history and the feel of that Saxon civilisation which has given England so many saints. Saint Aldhelm of Malmesbury became first Bishop of Sherborne when, in 705, it became for a time a cathedral town. Two brothers of Alfred the Great, Ethelbald and Ethelbert were buried there. It is even possible that Alfred himself was educated there, while Winchester was under Danish attack. It is certain that he visited the abbey on the Good Friday of 865 when his brother King

Ethelbert presented a charter to the community. And one very great figure of mediaeval times, St Stephen Harding, had his beginnings here when, born near by, he was offered while quite a child by his parents as an oblate to Sherborne Abbey. This was the man who, with St Bernard, became co-founder of the Cistercian Order at Cîteaux.

So Sherborne is full of history and, though the beautiful abbey is Norman, the echoes of that saint-filled Saxon world from which it sprang are somehow still to be heard. It has its treasures, too. The Sherborne Missal, one of the finest English mediaeval illuminated manuscripts known, was produced here and, though the original, curiously enough, is now kept at Alnwick Castle, the home of the Duke of Northumberland, a facsimile of it can be seen in the museum. So also should many other things in this evocative place, from the amazing fan vaulting in the nave and choir of the abbey to the attractive curving little streets around. Not surprisingly, many modern pilgrims come to Sherborne.

So also do they go to Shaftesbury, and rightly so, for here was once, in the shrine of Edward the Martyr, a pilgrim centre of great wealth and importance. Indeed, so great was this wealth, that there was once an old saying to the effect that if the Abbot of Glastonbury married the Abbess of Shaftesbury, their son would be richer than the King himself.

But these splendours which once were Shaftesbury's have now to be sought for. Of the great abbey nothing now remains but ruins among the grass. When I was there excavations were in progress and without a doubt there is much yet to be discovered in and about this place. Once there were no less than eleven churches here; but now St Peter's is the only ancient building still standing. Yet this 'Saxon town on a hill' as a notice outside the place describes it, has much to say to today's pilgrim, provided that he is prepared, in a leisurely exploration, to let the place speak for itself.

King Alfred built it, or rather fortified an existing strong point. Here he founded an abbey, unusually for that time, building it of stone, and made his daughter the first Abbess. The nuns of Shaftesbury became influential figures in the Middle Ages, and among them was an ancestress of John Wesley. But it was a murder which brought fame and fortune to Shaftesbury Abbey.

In the 1930s, when the ruins of Alfred's abbey were being excavated, some bones, almost certainly those of Edward, King and martyr, slain at Corfe Castle and later enshrined here, were discovered. This Edward, son of King Edgar, ruled England for three years before his brutal death. It took place, in a dramatic scene, by the lodge of the castle, where Edward, thirsty and mud-stained from the hunt, had called for refreshment. As he drank a cup of wine which his stepmother Elfride, who was deeply jealous of her stepson, handed to him, one of her servants, on her orders, stabbed him in the back. Mortally wounded, the King galloped away but, as he slipped from the saddle, his foot caught in the stirrup and he was dragged along the ground. But Elfride felt contrition for the dead and in retribution gave rich gifts for the abbey at Shaftesbury which held the body of the murdered man. Soon miracles were reported as occurring there: the fame of it spread. Edward was made saint and martyr, and by 1001 a shrine was created in the church for him and his relics, probably those very same discovered in the leaden casket in the 1930s, were visited by pilgrims for centuries, making their way up to Shaftesbury from the great plain below, which can now be seen so clearly from the terrace flanking the abbey ruins.

Salisbury and St Osmund

Inevitably, Salisbury's famous spire, best seen from across the River Avon, just as the painter Constable viewed it, dominates the mind just as it does the whole magnificent spectacle of this cathedral from the outside. As an architectural masterpiece it is not easily surpassed: its exterior overpowering, its interior very beautiful. But for anyone who goes there, as I did, to seek out the rich memorials of the past, and to tread in the steps of the pilgrims it can at first be a disappointment. Salisbury cannot and does not claim the rich historical associations of such a place as, say, Winchester, and the comparative absence, in tomb and chantry and other storied memorabilia of the past seems to underline this fact. In particular, Salisbury seems reticent about its saint, Osmund, which may be why he is so often passed by by those who, seeking more famous names, prefer to leave him aside. Even what remains of his shrine, the customary tomb with

Salisbury Cathedral, an architectural masterpiece not easily surpassed. (*A. F. Kersting*)

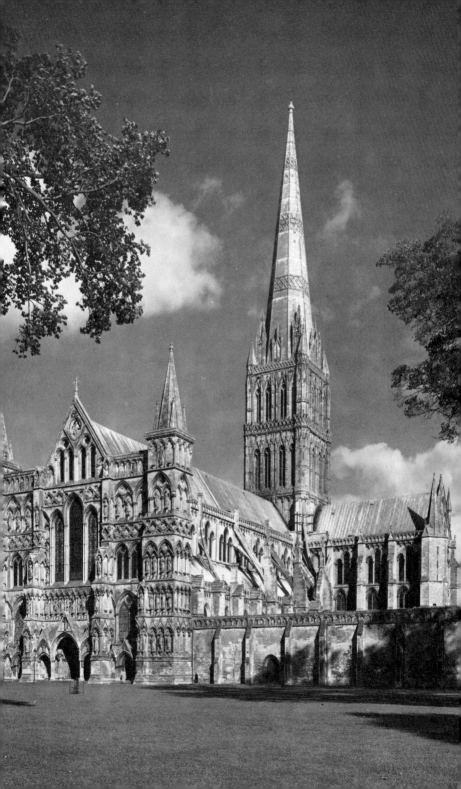

apertures in the side, lies tucked away in the South arcade of the nave, as though expressing a feeling that there was nothing further to be said about Osmund.

But there is. Not only is his story deeply interesting in itself, presenting a vivid picture of those dramatic years in England's history just after the Norman Conquest, but also leads, in an account of his canonisation process now available after many years in which the documents were lost, to a fascinating glimpse into the psychology of an age long past when such saints were made. So if Winchester can show us, as we shall discover when we get there, what pilgrims looked like, Salisbury in its story of St Osmund has much to say about how they thought.

Osmund was a Norman, closely related to the Conqueror, a member of his household and eventually his chancellor. After the victory at Hastings he crossed over in the wake of the army and in 1078, at the age of thirty-two, became Bishop of Sarum. It is not really possible to understand Salisbury as it is now, without visiting Old Sarum, that extraordinary and rather forbidding place of ruins high on its hill some 2 miles north of the present cathedral. Originally it was an early Iron Age fortified town. The Romans used it in their turn as a fortress and communication centre and the Normans rebuilt the defences and crowned them with a castle. This was the place to which Osmund, already possessed of a reputation for sanctity as well as ability, came as bishop, there creating a cathedral the foundations of which can still be seen. It was an extremely uncomfortable place to inhabit: short of water – this was one of the reasons for its eventual abandonment – cold and windy. Around the fortress, and spilling out upon the plain below, was a small town largely inhabited by Saxons now conquered and oppressed. To the Normans these were essentially an inferior race: primitive, credulous even childlike. For Osmund, their new bishop, dwelling among them in primitive surroundings until his cathedral could be built, they were the object of his greatest love and care.

Memories have survived of a visitation of his enormous diocese which he undertook shortly after taking up office, so that he can be seen in imagination leading his little party, he on horseback, they on foot, through the forests and marshes of the great country around: visiting hidden hamlets and isolated clergy and the religious houses of that old Saxon England, going to them not as a conqueror but as a brother in Christ. He was able to encourage and restore the spiritual life of some of these religious houses, including Shaftesbury, and Wimborne, Sherborne and Wareham. And all the time, between these various journeys, he was active in Sarum in building up the life of the community centred upon his new cathedral. When he died, in 1099, notable tributes were paid to him. Anselm, Archbishop of Canterbury, said he was 'the friend of God'. William of Malmesbury said of him 'this is a man free of all reproach'. Centuries later, a Benedictine congregation at Saint-Maur, in the Normandy of his birth, made a record of his life and writings adding: 'If we seem to have been somewhat eulogistic in our account of this great Bishop, our excuse is that no one hitherto has gone to the trouble of making known to all what Osmund was, and what he continues to be.' Osmund was buried in his cathedral at Sarum, remaining there until, in 1226, he was taken to the new cathedral which by that time Bishop Richard Poore had created, having been granted by the Pope permission to move out of Old Sarum, with its many hardships and disadvantages, to a new site on the plain below. Shortly afterwards permission was sought from Rome for a canonisation process for Osmund to begin. Permission was granted and the immense task was actually completed, signed and sealed not long afterwards. But it was never delivered in Rome because Bishop Poore, who had instigated it all, was sent to be Bishop of Durham. And so the documents remained for a long, long time forgotten among the cathedral records. The process was not renewed until 1424. The climax of the whole affair came when, in 1457 in St Peter's Rome, Osmund was pronounced a saint 'to be venerated by all the faithful and by the Universal Church'.

It is the documents connected with this two-stage process of canonisation which provide such a vivid glimpse into the minds of those at that time seeking it. Evidence of miracles connected with the desired saint had to be attested before commissioners and sworn on oath. Fifty-two miracles were thus attested before the commissioners for the canonisation process of Osmund. Almost all are connected with healing miracles, and those especially dating from the time when he was Bishop at Old Sarum, show both how vividly the Saxon peasantry remembered their bishop, and how prone they were, with a childlike faith, to see the miraculous in everything.

There was for instance, Simon of Wareham, who, seeking employment came to lodge in Old Sarum with a man called

Sampson the tanner. Simon became stricken with disease. A paralytic, he was removed by his landlord to lie in the open before the gate of the castle. In this sad situation he was visited by Bishop Osmund in a vision and was told to go to his tomb in the cathedral. They laid him on it and the man was healed. Another case, reminiscent of the humour to be found quite often in mediaeval wood-carvings, concerned one of the clergy of the cathedral who had the habit of sitting on Osmund's tomb. When he complained of a great pain in his head his attention was drawn to this habit. So he desisted, and immediately his pain went. Another man, this time a sacristan, testified to seeing Bishop Osmund in the night-time ascending to the altar, evidence which strengthened that given by a woman who said that she had seen lights about the tomb when the cathedral was in darkness. Then there was a boy named John who, having fallen into a cesspit, was thought to be dead till the body was taken to the sacred tomb, where it was revived. Similarly Thomas, a madman with shackled hands, was taken to the tomb. When he placed his shackled hands within one of the apertures, he became sane at once. And so it goes on, a striking picture of the mental processes of the time when the saints were resorted to much as medical consultants are today. But it is a fact in this case of Osmund that miracles attested before the commissioners in 1228 all dated back to events which took place one and a half centuries before, when the Saxon peasantry in Old Sarum revered him.

How these long past tales of miracles, attested before commissioners long dead, came to be preserved is in itself a strange story. The ancient parchments, having been kept in the muniment room of the cathedral, were taken for repair and binding to the British Museum some time towards the end of the last century. Bound in volume form, they were then returned to Salisbury and vanished again, apparently without trace. They reappeared following the death of one of the cathedral dignitaries – a man rejoicing in the wonderful name of Archdeacon Sanctuary – whose library was in due course put up for sale. When his books were exhibited in a local shop a passer-by noticed among them the bound copy of the missing process of canonisation, which the dignitary presumably had borrowed from the library of the cathedral and, absent-mindedly, had laid

Winchester Cathedral. Here for centuries the shrine of St Swithun attracted many pilgrims who, after visiting, would set out upon the southern Pilgrim's Way to Canterbury to the shrine of St Thomas. (*A. F. Kersting*)

aside among his own shelves. These were bought back by the cathedral's chapter clerk and so returned to their original home.

Winchester and St Swithun

Winchester is a marvellous place, vibrant with history and happenings. When I was there, there was a street theatre performing in one of the pedestrian precincts, the players in mediaeval costume, the crowd they had gathered eager and appreciative. Everywhere there seemed to be visitors, as eager as this audience to see some of the many things which this town offers. King Alfred from his statue splendidly surveyed the scene: the roof of the cathedral – it has the longest nave in England – stretched itself out in the sun and beneath it, inside the building, people seemingly from the world over, like the pilgrims of former times, moved among its splendours.

To an extraordinary extent, Winchester is soaked in the past. It was a Celtic settlement before the time of Christ. The Romans, even when they first came to it, found it a prosperous place and proceeded to make it more so, as the centre for a road system stretching far and wide. It became the capital for the Saxon kings who founded the kingdom of Wessex: in the seventh century it became a cathedral city with the removal from Dorchester of the see which had originally been founded there by the saintly Bishop Birinus, who had brought the faith to Wessex. After the Conquest William had his court here and regarded it as his capital as much as London. 'Domesday Book' was kept here. Cardinal Beaufort, who played such a sinister part at the trial and execution of Joan of Arc, is buried in the cathedral: so is William of Wykeham, founder of the College of St Mary at Winchester, now one of the most famous schools in the world, Winchester College. Mary Tudor was married in the cathedral to Philip of Spain. Charles II had his court in what is now the Deanery, the study of which was once his throne-room, when plague drove him from London. There scarcely seems to have been any time in England's history when Winchester was not, somehow, in the forefront of it.

It was, as in a different way it still is, a very great pilgrim centre, the fame of which was built upon the reputation of its saint, Swithun. Although never canonised officially, his cult became one of the most popular in England. Indeed, until primacy of place was taken by the shrine of St Thomas of Canterbury, his was the most popular. Throughout the Middle Ages right up to the Dissolution it continued to be so, forming the first stage in a well-known double pilgrimage which could be undertaken, especially by pilgrims from the Continent, who would cross over to Southampton, make their way to Swithun at Winchester and then overland by the Southern Pilgrim's Way to Thomas at Canterbury. Thence they would turn south again to Sandwich or Dover and so back to the other side of the Channel. Who, then, was this Swithun?

Like Osmund of Salisbury, he was probably of noble birth. He was certainly born in Winchester, the capital of Wessex, and adviser to King Aethelwulf. Born the year 800, he saw Saxon England in one of its most tragic times, subject to the full fury of Viking raids. By the time he became nineteenth Bishop of Winchester he had seen a Danish fleet arrive at Southampton and had seen Winchester itself under attack. In these troubled times

Swithun emerged as a strong and a practical-minded leader of his people, and became a much-loved bishop. On the great screen behind the high altar in the cathedral today he is shown holding a bridge, indicative of the fact that he inspired the building of one over the River Itchen at the East gate of the city, having been moved to do so, it was said, by the plight of humble folk making their way to market and having to ford the waters. So Swithun, apart from being a very important statesman at court when the Saxon kingdom was fighting for its life, was also from the first very much a bishop of the people. They liked the way in which he would always go about on foot, being a humble and self-effacing man. They liked the way in which he would out of his own pocket contribute to charitable causes. He showed this humility for the last time when, at his death in 862, he asked that he should be buried not in the cathedral, or with any pomp and ceremony, but in the common churchyard at the north-west side of the Saxon Cathedral, as it then was. The site of this grave, it may be said, has been quite recently identified by archaeologists. The stone marking the place, surprisingly enough, is the gift of the city of Stavanger in Norway, where the cathedral is dedicated to St Swithun, a fruit of the mission enterprise of the English Bishop Reinald who founded a church there in honour of St Swithun. Stavanger itself was in the Middle Ages known as the town of St Swithun.

The Saint lay in his humble grave for just over a century until Archbishop Dunstan of Canterbury, together with Bishop Aetholwold of Winchester, wishing to honour him as a churchman and as one who had in his lifetime continued the great work of Birinus, decided to move the body into the old minster which had by that time become the Church of the Benedictine Order which Aetholwold had established there. Such a decision in high places was fortified by reactions on the popular level. Stories got about that the grave of Swithun had appeared for some time to be opening of itself. Cures were claimed for those who had lain on the ground near it. Visions were said to have come to people who in them had seen the Saint himself asking for translation. Whatever the causes, the body of Swithun was indeed exhumed, the bones placed in a 'feretory', or portable shrine and taken into the church.

The event, however, was attended by a curious circumstance which has had a lasting effect upon the whole St Swithun legend. A rainstorm began as soon as the grave was disturbed and continued for forty days and nights, as though the Saint himself were weeping at the disturbance of his remains, and at the honour which was about to be done to them, so much in contradiction to the essential humility of his nature. This was the origin of the belief, very much alive today, that if it rained on St Swithun's Day, which is the date of the translation on 15 July 971, it would continue to rain for forty days afterwards. If it is fine on St Swithun's Day, the good weather will continue for forty days. The persistence of this belief is quite extraordinary. Thus, Ben Jonson, writing at the end of the sixteenth century, could say: 'St Swithun, the fifteenth day, variable weather for the most part . . . why, it should rain forty days after. It was a rule held before I was able to hold a plough.' And John Gaye, creator of *The Beggar's Opera*, in the eighteenth century remarked in one of his poems that:

> Now if on Swithun's Feast the welkin lours,
> And every penthouse streams with hasty showers,
> Twice twenty days shall clouds their fleeces drain,
> And wash the pavement with incessant rain.

This, then, was the Saint who was soon attracting pilgrims in great numbers to his shrine. His cult was sufficiently strong even by the time of the appointment of Alphege to Canterbury as archbishop in 1006 for that prelate to take the head of Swithun as a precious gift with him from Winchester. A continuous succession of miracles were already taking place through the merits of St Swithun. A truly astonishing one, which would have made a prime news story today, and which was duly recorded in the Cathedral Annals, concerned Queen Emma, in the early years of the eleventh century, who had been accused of having an affair with Bishop Alwyn of Winchester. She was sentenced to trial by ordeal, which was to take the form of walking over nine red-hot ploughshares in the nave of the cathedral. The King was present, together with an immense gathering of the nobility and clergy. The nine red-hot ploughshares were placed in position: the Queen's shoes and stockings taken off and then, walking between two bishops, both of them in tears, she was taken towards her ordeal. A cry went up from the crowd: 'O St

'Walking between two Bishops, she was taken towards her ordeal.' (Queen Emma at Winchester.)

Swithun, St Swithun, help her!' The miracle then followed as, guided by the bishops, she walked over the red-hot metal unscathed.

To a quite unusual extent, Winchester is a place where it seems possible to see, in imagination, the pilgrims which once thronged the place, just as in those attested miracles in the canonisation process of Osmund of Salisbury it seemed possible to feel something of their thought processes. In Winchester pilgrims can be seen, for that matter, not only in imagination but in actuality. There are carved figures on the stall ends in the Lady chapel which are in fact portraits of pilgrims made by wood-carvers of the Middle Ages. They are quite fascinating: one, a chunky figure with a distinctly disagreeable expression, carries a thick staff. Others bear scrolls of Scripture; most have a purse hanging from the neck, and a scallop shell, the emblem of pilgrimage, in the hat. These are the kind of figures to have in mind when calling up to the mind's eye the streams of pilgrims which converged on Winchester and St Swithun's shrine for so many years. They would be of all classes; the richer would be on horseback, the poorer, and these the vast majority, would be on foot. Many would be lame, struggling along as best they could on crutch or stick; equally many would be sick, most would be simple folk and all would be animated by the ardent belief that, could they but attain the shrine of Swithun, their prayers would be answered, their penances discharged or their ills cured.

If they came from the South they would come up the Itchen Valley and would arrive at the hospital of St Cross, which was founded in 1136 by Bishop Henry of Blois. This hospice should without fail be seen by today's pilgrim to Winchester. In times past, as now, it was possible to knock at the door and ask for a dole of bread and ale, given free, as charity to pilgrims. This hospice, or almshouse, for thirteen old men, has an enormous chapel and is altogether a very curious place indeed. From this Hospice of St Cross the pilgrims would have been able to see, across the river, St Catherine's Hill with a Norman chapel on the top of it. And they might if especially devout, climb this hill and hold a service of thanksgiving in the chapel there. They would then descend into Winchester and, having booked lodging for the night at one of the many hostels, would go on to the cathedral. Here they would enter, joining a queue which would already have formed, by a door, the traces of which can still be seen, in the North transept. Once within the building the queue would make for the Chapel of the Holy Sepulchre, at the foot of a stairway leading up to the East end of the church and the shrine of Swithun. This chapel was dark and cavelike, as befitting its name: its altar glowed with many lights and above this altar were scenes of the Passion.

The shuffling line of pilgrims would go on next, marvelling as they did so at the richness of the carvings above and about them, to that which they had come so far to see, the feretra, or portable shrine of Swithun, in a wide space behind the high altar, still to be seen and now occupied, indeed, by a modern recreation of this feretory. In a room behind the great screen relics were displayed. By entering an arched doorway called 'the Holy Hole', pilgrims, by stretching out an arm, could touch the relics of the saint, after which they would make their way out by the same route through which they had entered. They would not be able to use the South transept because this was part of the area set aside for the Benedictine monks of the foundation who worshipped in the cathedral. They would, however, be able to peer through the beautiful Pilgrim gates, still there, and maybe see some of the monks within. Pilgrims would then seek out their night's lodging: for the better-off it might be in an inn; for women it would be probably in the Nunnaminster; for the poorer it might be just some floor to sleep on. Most would have in mind that, on the morrow, they would be leaving by the road which went out of the North gate of the city in order to make their way to an even greater shrine – the greatest in all England – that of St Thomas at Canterbury. To follow them there is the last stage of this journey.

CHAPTER 7

Canterbury and St Thomas

The 'Pilgrim's Way'

Strictly speaking, there is no such thing as a 'Pilgrim's Way', between Winchester and Canterbury, even though many made the journey between those two points and even though an actual route is marked on the Ordnance Survey map. But this route, stretching for 112 miles, viewed as a continuous track, has no historical foundation and owes a good deal to the imagination of Hilaire Belloc who walked it in eight days in the winter of 1899, aiming to reach Canterbury on 29 December, on the 729th anniversary of the martyrdom in the cathedral there of Thomas Becket. His book *The Old Road*, published in 1910, tells of the matter. The title is significant: Belloc to some degree identified the Pilgrim's Way of later centuries with the infinitely older route along the chalk uplands followed by prehistoric man moving to and fro across southern England, avoiding, as far as possible, the dense forests which covered the lowlands and leaving behind him traces of his passage such as the megalithic ruins known as Kit's Coty House in Kent. Even so, pilgrims certainly did make their various ways between Winchester and Canterbury throughout the Middle Ages, drawn by the magnet of the enormously widespread and influential cult of St Thomas. Henry II himself must have gone that way when, within a very few years of the martyrdom, he made his own penitential pilgrimage, having landed at Southampton, to the tomb of 'the holy, blisful martyr'. What is more, there are along whole stretches of this way plenty of indications that it was heavily used, by drovers and merchants and all the other variegated traffic of the Middle Ages, as well as by pilgrims. What they certainly did not do was travel upon one single, clearly marked trackway.

Continental pilgrims, especially Bretons and Normans, crossed to Southampton and made their way to Winchester in order to make the circular trip, as was mentioned earlier, taking in the shrine of Swithun at Winchester, then to that of Thomas at Canterbury and so back across the Channel by way of Dover or Sandwich or other of the Channel ports.

What does clearly delineate the route generally taken by pilgrims between Winchester and Canterbury are the churches, abbeys, resting-places and other traces of their passage strung out like gems on a thread all the way between the two ancient places.

The martyrdom of Becket

Thomas à Becket, Archbishop of Canterbury, met his death in his cathedral from a smashing sword blow to the head on 29 December 1170. It was the afternoon of a day made dark not only by mid-winter but also by the particularly heinous nature of the crime – an act of sacrilege made even more terrible both by the sanctity of the victim and the holiness of the place. Within days the news had spread. When the King, Henry II, heard of it he shut himself up for three days, and was heard crying aloud that he was not responsible. The Pope for a time refused to receive any Englishman in audience. And almost immediately miracles were reported, not only in Canterbury, around the burial-place in the crypt where the monks had placed the body, but also further afield. Only two days after the killing, a Gloucester girl was cured of a head complaint after praying to the martyr. A knight, William Belet, in Berkshire was cured of a swelling in the arm. The cult and the fame of Becket, destined to last so long, and indeed never to fade away, had come into being.

But Canterbury was already a famous place. An important Roman centre, it had also prehistoric origins. In the Christian history of England it became, as it has remained, beyond compare. Augustine came here to convert Ethelbert of Kent in 597, and, long before ever it reached the Gothic splendours of the present, was a centre for pilgrimage. It held the bodies of St Alphege, the Archbishop slain by the Danes, of Anselm and Dunstan. It held the heads of three other saints and the arms of eleven more. It also possessed a portion of the true Cross, a thorn from Christ's crown, Aaron's rod, wool woven by the Blessed Virgin and also some of the clay out of which God made Adam. Holy relics were therefore no new things in this old place when

A portable reliquary as used to contain saintly relics. This splendid example, probably made in Limoges about 1195, held relics of St Thomas of Canterbury. A scene from his martyrdom is depicted on the side. This reliquary may have been made for Peterborough, as the Abbot took relics of St Thomas there in 1177. In 1979 it was sold at Sothebys for £462,000. (*The Guardian*)

those of Becket came to be added to their number.

But the martyrdom of Becket was something special, arising out of the clash between two strong and yet dramatically different characters, Becket himself and the King who, in the earlier part of his life he devotedly followed, Henry II. Henry, whose effigy on his tomb at Fontevrault in France shows a deceptively placid face, was a tumultuous character, one of the most alarming of the Plantagenet kings. Lecherous, violent, impious, with a pock-marked face and an eye that could strike terror, and surrounded by an entourage of brutal henchmen, he was at the same time formidably shrewd.

Becket was a more involved character: so involved, so, in a sense, mysterious, so many-sided, that his personality has continued to intrigue writers and artists. The thirteenth-century stained glass portrait of him in one of the cathedral's windows, thought to have been executed by someone who knew him, shows a very remarkable face indeed. And in this twentieth century, T. S. Eliot, among others, felt drawn to explore the proud, difficult and complicated character of this man upon whose body, when the attendant priests stripped him after his death, a verminous hair shirt was found and was once exhibited, among the furniture of his shrine.

He was born in London in 1118, the son of a merchant, Gilbert, who had originated in Normandy. His mother, Matilda, probably came from Caen, and was the only woman in the life of Thomas to arouse his affections. The power of Thomas, an aspect of his fascination, to arouse legends about himself after his death, is reflected in a story once current about his mother. According to this, she was a Saracen princess whom Gilbert Becket met when, having gone on crusade to the Holy Land, he was taken prisoner and fell in love with his captor's daughter. When he escaped and made his way back to London she followed after him, having only two words of English, 'London', and 'Becket'. With only these two words she reached London, found her fiancé, who then married her. The result was Thomas Becket.

Like so many of his class and type, he was as European as he was English. He was educated in Paris after being at school at the Priory of Merton in Surrey. The service of the Church attracted him early, much as the service of the State might attract a promising young man into the higher branches of the Civil Service now. Clever and eloquent, he attracted the attention of his peers and, shortly after joining the household of the Archbishop of Canterbury, Theobald, he was sent to continue his education in Italy and later in France again. Early in his career, therefore, he was put in touch with men and affairs and, when Henry II came to the English throne in 1154, at the age of twenty-one, the paths of two outstanding men of their times at last met. Becket, at the suggestion of Archbishop Theobald, became chancellor to King Henry, a position which made it possible for him to display his qualities and also to enjoy power and privilege to a marked degree. He developed, too, a close friendship with the King, learnt how to meet his dangerously changing moods, and enjoyed, as a consequence, particular favours from him. He even, at one stage of his career, had what amounted to almost a private army, and indeed fought with it in France.

This, then, was the brilliant man who, from being in importance the second man in the kingdom, came eventually to be on a collision course with the monarch he had served so closely. It was a disturbed time, and a brutal one. In England, as elsewhere in Europe, there were two power sources within the State: Church and Crown. Of liberty, in the sense of each man being able to go his own way, there was very little. A strong king, such as Henry II, could be a dictator whose absolute powers could be curtailed, if they ever were to be, by the Church. It was out of this fact that Becket's subsequent popularity as in some sense a champion of the people against the tyranny of the Crown, came to be. Yet for a long time, even when Archdeacon of Canterbury, Becket frequently took the King's part in disputes, such as that which arose over the privileges of Battle Abbey. In this, as in other related matters, such as the support of what many felt to be unjust taxation, he openly supported the King. In return, Henry treated him with the utmost favour, sending him on a glittering diplomatic mission to France to arrange the marriage of a French princess to the young Prince Henry.

Then came a dramatic change. When Archbishop of Canterbury Theobald died, Henry nominated Thomas as his successor. It was a post of enormous importance: in the absence of the monarch the archbishop of the day would administer the whole country and this indeed is what Theobald had done during the frequent absences of Henry in France. Now, in the May of 1162, Thomas Becket was ordained priest and eight days later consecrated bishop and enthroned as Archbishop of Canterbury. From then on, gradually but inexorably, his allegiances changed and he became, in many crucial matters, an opposer of the royal will. It was really a matter of ultimate allegiance, and in this area many have seen the true drama of Becket. Church or State, God or mammon: to which does a man owe his ultimate loyalty? Becket decided for the Church of which, in England, he was the head, and from this stemmed that train of events which ended in the place of his martyrdom on that dark December day of 1170.

Becket opposed the King in the matter of the power of the King's courts over against the Church courts, an issue which, thus baldly stated, seems arid enough, but which was in fact of tremendous importance, since the right of Church courts to try their own was an important hedge against the unbridled power of the Crown. Becket opposed the King in the whole matter of royal authority, as laid down in the Constitutions of Clarendon which emerged from a council called by Henry in 1164 in an effort to solve the growing number of points at issue between himself and his people. Summoned to a royal council at Northampton to defend himself against an infuriated King, Becket stood firm in spite of every provocation. It was shortly after this that he crossed over to France, to remain there in self-imposed exile for six years, putting himself under the protection of the King of France. Many times Henry tried to be reconciled with him. At other times he subjected Becket's helpless dependants to the most brutal treatment, dispossessing and imprisoning them. For his part Becket did not hesitate to use the dreaded weapon of excommunication and at one time suspended such distinguished prelates as the Archbishop of York and the Bishops of London and Salisbury. Eventually, perhaps believing that some reconciliation was possible, perhaps feeling that he was going to an inevitable end, Becket returned to England, landing at Sandwich and going straight to Canterbury along a way lined with welcoming people. On Christmas Day in the cathedral he preached upon the text, 'Peace on Earth, and goodwill to men', at the same time telling the congregation that they would soon have another martyr to join Alphege who centuries before in that place had been slain by the Danes. The King was now in Normandy and to him there went men, including the suspended bishops, who incited him to anger by accounts of what they represented as the insurrectionary activities of Becket. Flying into one of his sudden rages, Henry uttered his famous cry, demanding to know if there was no one who would rid him of this 'turbulent priest'. Four knights took him at his word: Reginald Fitz-Urse, William de Tracy, Hugh de Moreville and Richard Brito. They crossed to England, were soon joined by an odious character called Ranulf de Broc who had been in charge of the persecutions of Becket's household in his absence, and immediately pressed on to Canterbury. This was now 29 December. The party arrived about 3 p.m., going firstly to confront Becket in his palace where he was

'The three knights attacked the Archbishop at the altar.' (Murder of Becket.)

with his household. They cursed him, demanding that he should declare obedience to the King in all respects, and do all that was expected of him. He refused with much constancy and the knights armed themselves. Meanwhile Thomas had been persuaded by his clergy to enter the cathedral where Vespers were being sung. Into that shadowy, stone-columned interior the knights followed him, calling him a traitor to the King. After a short struggle Becket was dispatched by three sword blows, the first from Fitz-Urse to the head, the next which was partly shielded by one of his attendants, the third which struck him down. A final and fourth blow cut off the whole of the top of his skull, spilling his brains upon the stone floor. Then, after a short time of plundering in the palace, the knights returned to Saltwood Castle.

The monks who had been with Becket now crept out of their hiding-places, reverently gathered up the body, together with the blood and brains, and carried it on a bier to the high altar. It was later entombed by them in the crypt where it remained until the great translation of 7 July 1220, and, because de Broc had threatened to desecrate it, it was from the first protected by a heavy stone slab. Such, then, was the martyrdom. There are perhaps two reasons why the news of it spread with such extraordinary rapidity. Firstly, the conflict between Becket and his King had been watched for years with fascinated attention all over Europe, a cause of whispered talk in many a cloister and court. The murder was therefore news of the first order, and spread along the Church's lines of communication. But also from the very first this martyrdom had its reporters and Becket his biographers. No death and no saint and no cult in history, certainly not in England, was anything like as fully reported upon as this one. It was a monk named Benedict, who had been nearby at the time of the murder, who was subsequently placed in charge of the relics and given an especial concern to those who came seeking miraculous healings. His is the first record of the miracles performed by St Thomas, who was officially canonised by the Pope in 1173, only three years after his death. These many and extraordinary miracles recorded by Benedict give a preview of what was to happen in later centuries, when healing powers of Chaucer's 'holy blisful martyr' exceeded in fame all others.

A blacksmith in nearby Thanet was cured of his blindness – one of the windows in the Trinity chapel in Canterbury Cathedral illustrates this miracle and shows how he later offered gold pieces at the shrine in gratitude. There was a madman who, dragged kicking and screaming to the tomb and kept there all through the night, was sane in the morning. There was a woman in Dover who slept by the tomb all night and was cured of an interior complaint. There was a young man in Northampton, a sufferer from some kind of gastro-enteritis, who was likewise cured at the place where Thomas lay. The miracle which befell a London shoemaker suffering with a fistula illustrates a feature of cures through the medium of St Thomas which was to become intercontinentally famous: the man drank some of the water which could be obtained in Canterbury and which was held to contain, infinitely diluted, some of the saint's blood. It was the properties of this water which led to the ampoules, or small containers, sometimes worn as jewellery, which were bought by pilgrims to the shrine all through its history, and which would be taken back home as proof of a pilgrimage accomplished and possibly as a gift to some suffering relative who would be allowed a drop of the precious water.

The monks, who had first taken the body to the high altar, later placed it in the crypt and secured it with the slab as a protection against the possibility of its being disturbed. This tomb in the crypt had the customary openings in the sides, such, for instance, as with the case of the tomb of St Oswald in Salisbury or St Wite in that little church at Whitchurch Canonicorum. This is the reason why the amazing windows in the Trinity chapel in the cathedral, which depict whole series of miracles at the shrine, show it as of this form, rather than that of the sumptuous shrine which, after 1220, it had assumed. Therefore pilgrims kneeling at this great shrine would, on looking around in the Trinity chapel, see these stories of miracles, marvellously illustrated, as taking place around a tomb of the earlier and simpler kind.

There is nothing like these windows, and the tales they tell, anywhere else in England. Here, clearly visible even on a dull day of winter, are illustrated in wonderful richness and variety of colour, some of the happenings which earlier ages devoutly believed to have happened, and which reflect the simpler faith of a day gone by. There is the story of the Rochester boy, named Robert, who fell into the River Medway and, being taken out, could on no account be revived. In that lamentable condition he lay until his mother, distraught, vowed to St Thomas silver thread of the length of the boy's body, whereupon he recovered. So, in one of these wondrous windows of the Trinity chapel, boys can be seen on the banks of the river throwing stones at frogs until one of them falls in. A second medallion shows the boys running to tell the parents. A third shows them grieving on the river bank as the corpse is pulled out.

Some of the miracles illustrated in these windows are detailed and lengthy, such as those experienced by a knight called Jordan FitzEisulf. It is important to have the sequence of events here before the details can be picked out in the window. Plague kills the knight's son and also the boy's nurse, whose funeral is depicted. So is the death of the boy, so also is the arrival of twenty pilgrims from Canterbury who carry some of the water of St Thomas, which is able to revive the child. But the money placed in the boy's hands as an offering of thanks to St Thomas for this relief, under a vow that it should be presented to St Thomas before mid-Lent, never reaches its destination, the vow being forgotten. At this point the Saint appears to a leper called Gimp who warns Jordan of the danger of this oversight. Again the promise is broken and this time the knight's eldest son is stricken and dies. Filled with remorse, and themselves ill, Jordan and his wife hasten to Canterbury to ask forgiveness at the shrine. All these incidents, concluding with that in which Jordan at last places his offering at the sacred tomb, can be picked out in this part of this window, which can be found on the north side of the Trinity chapel.

Some of these miracles are on the grand scale. There is one commemorative window showing Becket appearing to King Louis VII of France, to which is attached a moving and true story. In 1179 this King had cause to plead to St Thomas for the recovery of his son, stricken with illness. He crossed to England – the first French king ever to do so – passed a whole night in prayer at the tomb and, in thankfulness for the eventual recovery of his son, presented to the shrine the most amazing jewel, known as the regale of France, a great ruby which glowed thereafter for centuries among the riches of the shrine and indeed was its most famous possession. Henry VIII, after the Dissolution and the plundering of the shrine, wore it as a ring on his thumb, after that his daughter, Mary Tudor, wore it in a golden collar, and thereafter it vanished.

Many kings made their way to St Thomas. Henry II himself, filled with remorse, walked barefoot from the West gate of the city to the tomb in the crypt, having dismounted at Harbledown. At the tomb he permitted himself to be scourged, an act notable

'The monks scourged King Henry at the tomb of St Thomas.' (Henry II at Canterbury.)

for a king but not unique among pilgrims, for whom it was a regular practice as the expiation of a penance, to allow themselves to be thus beaten with rods by the attendant clergy. Later, Richard Lionheart, one of Henry's sons, came here to thank God and St Thomas for the safe return from overseas, and John came here for his coronation. In the fullness of time it came to pass that almost every English monarch in his turn climbed those worn steps up to the shrine which stands there still.

The pilgrims

But what happened to pilgrims when, whether like Chaucer's party in early spring, or like the thousands who would come for the Feast of the Translation in July, or those hardier souls who came to Canterbury for the annual commemoration of the

The approach to Canterbury. This is the view which pilgrims from London and Rochester, such as Chaucer's party, would have had as they descended the hill from the village of Harbledown. (*Fisk-Moore Studios, Canterbury*)

martyrdom in December, they approached down the hill from Harbledown into the walled city? The one entry to this wall which is still standing is West gate, and I found it rewarding to walk thoughtfully from there through the streets to the cathedral, conjuring up along the way the sights and sounds which would have been encountered by those pilgrims. All through the year they would have been coming; only at those two particular seasons would there have been a greater crowd than usual. If they were a mounted party, they would have been moving along, for the greater part of their journey, at a canter, an ambling trot which was the name used to describe it, and which has given a word to the language, just as Canterbury bells, the name of a flower, was used for the little bells which hung on their bridles and gave a characteristic sound.

178 ·

There would be a huge din as they entered the city, the cries of trades-people clamouring for their custom, the shouts of inn-keepers, of hawkers peddling innumerable tourist trinkets and the pipes and voices of wandering troupes of entertainers. The old buildings on either side would contain, as indeed they still do, many reminders that this was a pilgrim city, a hospice for aged priests, an almshouse for aged poor, houses of the religious orders and pilgrim lodges of all sorts. Chaucer's party stayed at an inn called 'Chequers of the Hope' which had 100 beds, probably all in one single dormitory. This building still stands, although it is not an inn it bears the title still. And so the pilgrims would make their way to hospitals, to convents, some, especially if they were poor, to the Strangers' Hall, now a part of the King's School. The wealthier would walk down a covered passageway known as the Pentise, part of which is to be seen now in the garden of one of the school boarding-houses. That would lead them into the Cellarer's Hall, where the Archdeacon of Canterbury now lives, and where there are still chambers called Paradise and Heaven. Very distinguished visitors would occupy the house called 'Meister Omers', still there.

The majority of pilgrims, who on entering the city would find themselves excitingly mingled with others from all over Europe, would be exposed to the full blast of tourist trade. Some idea of how intrusive this could be is reflected in a by-law which once existed and which stated that: 'No Inn Keeper or Host, when any pilgrims or strangers come to the city, shall catch them by their reins, their clothing or their staves and try to make them come into his Inn, nor shall any cross over the thresholds of his Inn when shouting at the said pilgrims and strangers passing along, inviting him in, under pain of imprisonment or fine.' They would be especially importuned as they passed down the Mercery, the narrow street still there leading to what is now the entry to the cathedral precincts. In the Mercery every conceivable article of tourism would be on offer, the vendors holding them up before the eyes of the wondering pilgrims, necklaces for holding the ampoules of the water of St Thomas, badges, pins, all sorts and manner of memento, some of which can be seen to this day in the Cathedral Exhibition in the undercroft.

As I walked along Mercery Lane, thinking of all this, I was reminded of that curious ballad or poem written in the fifteenth century and called *The Tale of Beryn*, which purports to be some kind of a sequel to Chaucer, and to describe what his pilgrims did when they had found their lodgings for the night. They certainly bought their mementoes, quite possibly in this very Mercery

> But first, as manner and custom is, pilgrim signs they bought;
> For men from home should know the Saint whose shrine
> they have sought.
> Each man laid out his silver in the things that he liked best.
> They set their tokens on their heads, some on their caps did
> pin,
> Then to the dinner-ward went back to their Inn.

Very much in character, after the meal, the Knight took his son to inspect the battlements of the town, the Wife of Bath being fatigued, invited the Prioress to walk with her in the garden and have a little drink of wine; the Miller and the Cook went elsewhere to drink a great deal more, the Pardoner went out into the town to find a woman.

But all, high or low, virtuous or villainous, would make for the Cathedral and its enormously famous shrine.

The shrine

Those who entered the cathedral in the high noon of mediaeval pilgrimage, as did Chaucer's party, would have found themselves in a building of surpassing beauty, created largely – after a series of rebuildings and extensions following a great fire in 1067 – to be, after the murder of Becket in 1170, a fit setting for his shrine. It is true that they would not have seen the great Gothic nave as it is now, which was completed in 1410, or the famous stone pulpitum separating choir from nave, which is fifteenth-century work. But they would have been able to marvel at the building which was largely the creation of two inspired builders, William of Sens and his successor, William the Englishman, built of Caen stone brought over from Normandy.

Those pilgrims who came before the translation in 1220, would have three stations to visit at which reverence could be made to the Saint. Entering by the North transept door, through which Becket had gone to his death, they would, having been formed into a processional column, and led by a monkish guide, visit first the place of the martyrdom. There they would have found the

Altar of the Sword's Point, on the place of the murder and bearing the fragments of the broken sword of de Brito, the weapon which, cutting through Becket's skull, had broken on the stone floor. This altar has now gone – it vanished in 1539 – but there is a stone commemorative of the martyrdom and tens of thousands visit the place still. After this they would have gone up to the high altar, where the body had first lain. They would then have gone down to the crypt where there was the tomb and also a gold-mounted portion of the skull kept, which they would be invited to kiss as it was held out to them. After 1220, in addition to these holy places, there would be the corona, a circular tower at the East end which held, suitably mounted in gold and precious stones, the top of the skull which had been sliced off. But, beyond all other things in wonder, there was the shrine itself.

The Pilgrim's Steps up to the Trinity Chapel where the shrine of Becket, covered with jewels, stood on the left at the top. The steps have been worn by the feet of thousands of pilgrims through the centuries. The shrine was destroyed in 1538; but still pilgrims come in their thousands. The canopy at the top of the steps beyond the pillar covers the tomb of the Black Prince. (*Fisk-Moore Studios, Canterbury*)

This was approached up a series of gradually ascending levels, stairway after stairway, just as the area is now. At the head of these worn stone steps, surrounded by the marvellous windows of the Trinity chapel, and flanked by royal tombs, that of Henry IV on the north side and of the Black Prince on the south, was the shrine. Generations of great wealth had been poured out upon it: covered with plates of gold, it was also laden with precious jewels of all kinds – diamonds, emeralds, sapphires, rubies. At a sign from the monkish guide, the pilgrims would kneel – the marks on the tessellated floor where they did so may still be seen – and then he would raise on ropes the wooden cover displaying all this magnificence. Then, with a white wand, he would point out the more outstanding treasures, especially the regale, that ruby, gift of the King of France, in all its gleaming splendour.

After this supreme moment the pilgrims would be free to go their ways, although there were also other relics at hand in the cathedral which they could venerate and kiss if they so wished. When, years later, Erasmus and Colet visited the cathedral, they were offered the arm of St George with blood and flesh on it to venerate, which Colet, not surprisingly, refused to do. Also available were eleven arms, pieces of Christ's manger and also of his sepulchre and many other similar objects. Of Becket himself there were on view, for specially chosen pilgrims, his own vestments, now kept, incidentally, in the treasury of Sens Cathedral. And after that they could go their several ways, all wondering and some who had come with serious intent, rejoicing in another pilgrimage accomplished or, maybe, in a penance carried out. Wherever it was they came from, they would have much to tell when they returned.

So all through several centuries, from 1220 when, in a ceremony of the utmost magnificence, it was placed behind the high altar, right through to the end in 1539, it lay there; kings, prelates, nobles, cardinals and legates, together with countless ordinary folk, made their way to it. But, with the passage of time and the ebbing away of that kind of belief which had attracted so many for so long, the numbers dwindled. By the time of Henry IV there were critics to cast severe eyes on the practice of pilgrimage, as it had by that time come to be. 'I know well that when divers men and women will go after their own wills', said one Lollard, or follower of John Wycliffe and his teachings, when arraigned before Archbishop Arundel, 'and finding out a pilgrimage, they will order to have with them both men and women that can sing wanton songs; and some other pilgrims will have with them bagpipes, so that every town they came through, what with the noise of their singing and the sound of their piping, and with the jangling of their Canterbury bells, and with the barking of dogs after them, that they make more noise than if the King came that way.'

And yet in 1500, thirty-nine years before the end, a Venetian visitor was able to describe the shrine as he then saw it:

> The magnificence of the tomb of St Thomas the martyr, Archbishop of Canterbury, is that which surpasses all belief. This not withstanding its great size, is entirely covered over with plates of pure gold, but the gold is scarcely visible from the variety of precious stones with which it is studded. . . . And these beauties of nature are enhanced by human skill, for the gold is carved and engraved in beautiful designs, both large and small. . . . But everything is left far behind by a ruby not larger than a man's thumb nail, which is set to the right of the altar. The church is rather dark, and when we went to see it the sun was nearly gone down and the weather was cloudy; yet I saw that ruby as well as if I had it in my hand.

The sun finally went down upon this, as upon so many other shrines, and upon the old world in which they had played so important a part, with the arrival of the commissioners of Henry VIII to dismantle it. St Augustine's monastery at Canterbury was surrendered to the Crown on 30 July 1538, although the wearer of that crown, Henry VIII, had himself been present some years before at one of the great jubilee celebrations, held every fifty years, at the shrine. The confiscation was completed two years later, when it required twenty-six cartloads to take away the treasures. The bones of St Thomas were dispersed and no one has ever found where they are. It was at one time supposed that they had been discovered when, in 1888, a grave was opened in the crypt which was found to contain, among many bones, a skull bearing a large wound. To establish whether this were in fact that of Thomas, the cathedral authorities in 1949 had this exhumed and subject to expert examination. Alas, the verdict was that the wound had been caused by a spade, and that the remains were not those of Thomas. Perhaps it would have been surprising if they had been, for King Henry at the time of the destruction of the shrine had been anxious to remove any trace of anything connected with Thomas which encouraged people to reverence him. The royal proclamation said: 'From henceforth the said Thomas Becket shall not be esteemed, named, reputed, nor called a saint, but Bishop Becket and that his images and pictures through the whole realm shall be put down and avoided out of all churches, chapels and all other places. . . .' And that is the reason why, in St Albans Abbey at the very beginning of this journey, it was noted that the name of Becket had been 'mysteriously erased' from its place upon a pillar.

When I came out of the cathedral at the end of my visit, and indeed at the end of this journey, the autumn day was already fading. And in the gathering dusk it was difficult not to feel a moment of sadness for the vanished wonder world of pilgrim England which through so many generations had sent so many people up hill and down dale across the land to see its holy places. After all, they do add up to an astonishing and dramatic tale. There is St Alban, the Roman going to his death because some Christian priest had impressed him. There is St Etheldreda, presiding over that monastery far away in the Fens at Ely, and Mother Julian with her revelations of divine love, in her cell in Norwich, and Bromholm, with its vanished shrine of the Holy Rood in Norfolk, and Walsingham filled with pilgrims still. And there is Hugh of Lincoln with his swan, and at Beverley the lovable St John, upon whose grave the school-children still place primroses, and St William submerged in the splendours of York, and Wilfrid still represented in Ripon by a citizen riding through the town on a white horse once every year. Up in Northumberland, Cuthbert is still a potent influence in Durham and at Lindisfarne. In the Midlands the dark, mysterious crypt at Repton still keeps some of its secrets, Lichfield still speaks of St Chad, and astonishing Glastonbury draws as many, if not more, visitors as it ever has done. So, for that matter, does Winchester, and there are still many who follow their own particular Pilgrim's Way to Canterbury just as Chaucer's party did, so long ago, and with no doubt a similar mixture of motives.

So there is no real cause for sadness. For Pilgrim's England, as was said at the very beginning of this narrative, is alive and well and waiting still to show its wonders to whoever will seek them out.

Further Reading

The literature on pilgrimage is vast, so is that on particular saints. But for anyone wishing to make such a journey as is followed in this book, or to go further into the matter generally, the following will be found useful:

John Adair, *The Pilgrim's Way*. Thames and Hudson, 1978.
M. D. Anderson, *Looking for History in British Churches*. Murray, 1951.
The Anglo-Saxon Chronicle.
Bede, *A History of the English Church and People*, trans. L. Sherley Price. Penguin, 1968.
G. C. Coulson, *Mediaeval Panorama*. Cambridge University Press, 1940.
R. C. Finucane, *Miracles and Pilgrims*. J. M. Dent, 1977.
D. J. Hall, *English Mediaeval Pilgrimage*. Routledge and Kegan Paul, 1965.
F. Heer, *The Mediaeval World*. Weidenfeld and Nicolson, 1961.
S. Jennett, *The Pilgrim's Way from Winchester to Canterbury*. Cassell, 1971.
D. Rops, *The Church in the Dark Ages*. J. M. Dent, 1959.

The following short studies of particular saints are especially interesting:

The Quest for Alban, Arthur Swinson. Published by the Friends of St Albans Abbey.
The Venerable Bede, by C. J. Stranks. Published by SPCK.
The Life and Death of St Cuthbert, by C. J. Stranks. Published by SPCK.
St Etheldreda Queen and Abbess, by C. J. Stranks. Ely Cathedral Monographs.

St Hugh of Lincoln, by J. A. Froude. Recently republished by the Friends of Lincoln Cathedral.

St Wilfred of Ripon, by C. M. Wilkinson. The Wakeman Press, Ripon.

St Swithun, by F. Bussby. Published by the Friends of Winchester Cathedral.

The Story of St Osmund of Salisbury, by W. J. Torrance. Published by the Friends of Salisbury Cathedral.

Books about St Thomas of Canterbury are so numerous as to form a literature by themselves. Modern studies have included works by A. Duggan 1952, Nesta Pain 1964, D. Knowles 1970. T. S. Eliot's *Murder in the Cathedral* is a dramatic interpretation of Becket's character and of the events which led to his martyrdom.

Map of pilgrim shrines in England

Index

DATE DUE

GAYLORD			PRINTED IN U.S.A.